Primary Scie

for the Caribbean

. . . .

A Process Approach

. . . .

Book 5

Examination Preparation

Raphael Douglass   Trevor Garcia

Heinemann Educational Publishers
Halley Court, Jordan Hill, Oxford OX2 8EJ
a division of Reed Educational & Professional Publishing Limited

FLORENCE PRAGUE MADRID ATHENS MELBOURNE
AUCKLAND TOKYO SINGAPORE KUALA LUMPUR
JOHANNESBURG IBADAN GABORONE KAMPALA NAIROBI
PORTSMOUTH NH (USA) MEXICO CITY CHICAGO SÃO PAULO

British Library Cataloguing in Publication Data
A catalogue record for this book is available from the British Library.

Cover photograph by Roger Belix (Trinidad and Tobago)
Cover text and design by Gabriele Kern
Text and design by Gabriele Kern
Illustrated by Art Construction and B. L. Kearley Ltd

ISBN 0 435 043 455

Produced by **AMR** Ltd

Printed and bound in Great Britain by Scotprint Ltd, Musselburgh

97 98 99 10 9 8 7 6. 5 4 3 2 1

Publisher's acknowledgement
The publisher would like to thank Mrs Sitara Gardner of the Ministry of Education
for her advice and contribution to this book.

Authors' acknowledgements
Raphael Douglass would especially like to thank Mr Gordon Besson and Miss Joanne
Debasee of NIHERST, Mrs Sharon Mangroo and Miss Althea Maund of the Curriculum
Department of the Ministry of Education, and all the teachers who have been involved in
trials of the activities, as well as making and testing his low-cost apparatus. He would also
like to thank his daughter, Darlene, for her help on the series and his wife, Lucille, for the
help and inspiration she has given him. Trevor Garcia would like to thank his wife, Lucy,
for all her help and support with his work on this series.

Contents

Note: The topic and period numbers refer to the Primary Science Syllabus for Trinidad and Tobago (1994).

Preface

To the teacher

The new *Primary Science for the Caribbean* encourages pupils to form ideas, and to think for themselves. This book will help pupils achieve the aims and objectives outlined in the new Primary Science syllabus. Sections on the environment and on technology have been added, but the philosophy is still that of the *process approach: hands-on, minds-on.*

Co-operative learning is also introduced. Throughout the book, we emphasise *positive interdependence, individual accountability, shared responsibility for each other's learning, good working relationships and social skills.* Pupils are encouraged to work together in groups. We suggest you divide your class into groups of five. Groups should include pupils of mixed ability. Give each pupil specific duties, to achieve a particular goal or complete a task. You could give them the following roles:

- Principal investigator – leads group discussions
- Materials manager – responsible for collecting materials
- Recorder/reporter – records results and reports them to the class if asked
- Maintenance director – organises the cleaning up of the work area
- Liaison officer – communicates with the teacher if there are problems

Discuss with the pupils the tasks to be carried out for each of these roles. (See the Teacher's Guide for more about the co-operative approach.)

Key words are in **bold** and explained in the text. There is also a glossary at the back of the book to help pupils with some difficult words used in the text.

There is a Teacher's Guide, *How to Teach Primary Science – New Edition,* which accompanies the series. It gives guidelines on how to prepare for lessons, organise pupils for activities and assess pupils' progess. It also provides answers to questions and revision tests.

To pupils

This book will help you with your Primary Science. We hope you will enjoy doing the activities. By working with materials you will find answers from them. Sometimes you will work together as members of a team, helping each other and sharing responsibilities. You can all contribute ideas. Be friendly towards one another. Your science problems are problems to be solved by the group. If you have to criticise, criticise ideas, not other pupils.

Effect of Flowing Water on the Earth's Surface

Objectives

At the end of the chapter pupils should be able to

1 identify evidence of soil erosion resulting from flowing water (pages 6–8)

2 identify eroded material transported by flowing water (page 8)

3 identify soils that absorb water quickly and soils that absorb water slowly (pages 8–9).

You will be using a model to represent soil and rain. By watching what happens in your model, you can understand what happens in nature.

Activity 1   Rain falls on soil

Your group will need:

- 2 milk tins, open at both ends
- a teaspoon
- a large cake pan or box lined with plastic from a garbage bag
- 4 styrofoam cups — one with 10 small holes in the bottom made with the point of a pencil
- water
- a block of wood about 3 cm thick
- 2 sardine tins
- old newspaper
- a pencil

1 Collect two soil samples in the two tins (see the diagram). One soil sample must have grass growing on it. The other must just be bare soil.

Bring materials to school when asked

Safety!

- Make sure the edges of the tin are not sharp. Wash your hands after the activity.

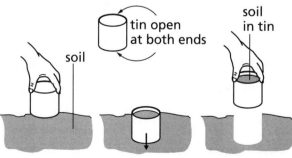

6

2 Gently knock the sample of bare soil out of the tin, so that it makes a mound in the pan. Slope the pan slightly by placing the block of wood under the pan near the mound of dirt.

cup with small holes in base

3 Discuss with your group what you think will happen when you pour water on to the soil in your model. This represents what would happen if rain fell on to some land on a hill. Write down your predictions to **a)** to **d)**.

   a) What will happen to the water as it falls on to the mound of soil?

   b) Will the water carry any soil down into the 'lake' at the bottom of the pan?

   c) If soil is carried down into the lake, what part of the mound will it come from? How much will be carried down?

   d) How fast will the water run down your model hill?

4 Pour a cup full of water into your cup with holes. Allow 'rain' to fall on your model hill. Observe what happens.

5 Scrape up any soil in the 'lake' with the spoon. Place it in a sardine tin. Label the tin. Leave it in the open for the water to **evaporate** (turn into water vapour and disappear into the air). You may have to leave it for a day or two. How much soil did the water carry away from the 'hill'?

6 Look at your group's predictions to **3 a)** to **d)**. Were your predictions very good, good, not so good? Make any changes to your predictions you need to as a result of your observations.

7 Repeat steps 2 to 6 above using the soil with the grass on it.

8 Write answers to the following questions in your notebooks.

   a) Which model hill lost more of its soil? Why did it lose more?

   b) In which model did water flow faster? Why?

9 Discuss what you think would happen if there was a heavier rain fall. You could try this out in your model by tipping out a cup of water over the soil in one go.

Fast moving water washes away **topsoil** (surface soil). This is called **soil erosion**. The faster the water moves over a slope the more erosion takes place. If you look at a steep hill that has no plants growing on it, you may see deep trenches where the soil has been eroded away.

We saw in Activity 1 that if there is grass on the soil, less soil is washed away. The roots of the grass hold the soil particles together. Cover crops such as grass, corn or soya beans slow down the speed of running water. This means less soil is washed away. More water soaks into the soil. The leaves of the cover crop plants break up rain drops. Thus the drops do not fall with much force on to the soil. This also helps to reduce erosion.

After heavy rain, rivers often appear very muddy. The water is full of eroded soil. The soil is **transported** (carried) by the running water to another place. When the water reaches a place where it runs more slowly, it leaves the soil behind. Soil that has been transported to another place is often the best agricultural soil. Sugar cane and bananas are grown for export on soil like this.

Activity 2 Soil that absorbs water

Your group will need:
- three long hollow containers (e.g. Cheers tubes joined together, see Teacher's Guide)
- samples of dry sand, loam and clay (enough to fill the containers)
- a margarine tub with water
- a styrofoam tray 14 cm × 21 cm
- scissors
- cotton wool
- ruler

1 Your teacher will give you some sand and some dried, ground-up clay and loam.

2 Plug the lower end of each tube with cotton wool.

3 Pack the three long tubes with equal amounts of soil (one with sand, one with loam, one with clay). Keep knocking the tubes on your desk while filling, so you can pack the tubes fairly tightly.

4 Stand the tubes in the tub of water, as shown in the diagram. Observe the tubes every ten minutes for half an hour.

5 Observe them morning and afternoon for the next six days. Discuss your observations with your group. Copy and complete Table 1 below.

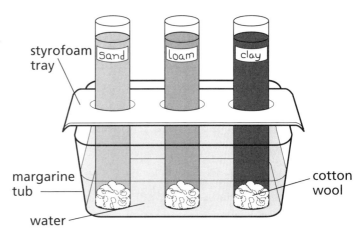

Table 1

Day	Time	Height of water in the tube (cm)		
		sand	loam	clay
1	0 min			
	10 min			
	20 min			
	30 min			
2	a.m.			
	p.m.			

5 Discuss the information in Table 1. Answer **a)** to **d)**.

  a) Which soil absorbed (soaked up) the most water after ten minutes?

  b) Which soil absorbed the least water after ten minutes?

  c) Which soil absorbed the most water after half an hour?

  d) Which soil absorbed the least water after twenty-four hours?

A loam soil contains **humus**. Humus helps soil to hold water and provides food for plants. Humus in topsoil will slow down the movement of water and reduce erosion.

Summary

- When heavy rain falls on ground that is not protected, topsoil (surface soil) is eroded. The valuable topsoil is washed away by the rain.
- Topsoil may be protected from erosion by planting cover crops such as grass and soya beans. The roots of these plants hold the soil particles together and help the soil to absorb (soak up) water. The leaves of the cover crop plants break up rain drops. Thus the rain drops do not fall with much force on to the soil. This also helps to reduce erosion.
- The humus in topsoil helps the soil to hold water. As water soaks into the topsoil humus, the speed of water flow is reduced. This reduces erosion.
- Removal of the topsoil by erosion reduces soil fertility. The soil below the surface, the subsoil, has very little humus.

Test yourself

For each task write down **A**, **B**, **C** or **D**.

1 Two farmers X and Y did not grow any crops on their land for about one year. Farmer X allowed some grass to grow on his land. Farmer Y kept his land bare in order to rest his land. Which prediction would you make?

A Farmer X's land would be in a good condition for the next crop.

B Farmer Y's land would be in a good condition for the next crop.

C Neither Farmer X's nor Farmer Y's land would be in a good condition for the next crop.

D Both Farmer X's and Farmer Y's land would be in a good condition for the next crop.

(Objective 1)

2 Farmer Brown says that soils transported by water are often very good agricultural soils. Farmer Kamal says that soils transported by water are water-logged and useless.

A Both Farmer Brown and Farmer Kamal are correct.

B Neither Farmer Brown nor Farmer Kamal is correct.

C Farmer Brown is correct.

D Farmer Kamal is correct.

(Objective 2)

3 A loam soil reduces erosion because

   A it absorbs much of the water flowing over it

   B it is a fertile soil

   C sugar cane and bananas grow well on a loam soil

   D farmers do not grow crops in a loam soil.

(Objectives 1 and 3)

4 You might infer that soil erosion had taken place after a heavy shower if you saw that the water had washed down

   A garbage

   B boulders

   C topsoil

   D shrubs and grasses.

(Objective 2)

5 Ryan filled three tubes with different soils. He pushed a piece of cotton wool into the bottom end of each tube and placed all the tubes in a trough of water. After 10 minutes he observed that the water level was

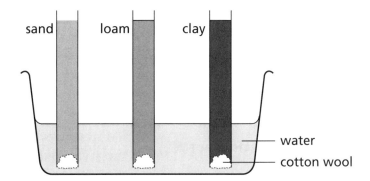

   A higher in the sandy and clay soils than in the loam soil

   B higher in the clay and loam soils than in the sandy soil

   C higher in the sandy and loam soils than in the clay soil

   D higher in the clay soil than in the sandy and loam soils.

(Objective 3)

Solar Energy

Objectives

At the end of the chapter pupils should be able to

1 identify suitable materials that can be used for solar energy transfer (pages 12–14)

2 identify and state ways in which solar energy can be used in the home (pages 14–15)

3 observe and state that an open system will collect less heat energy from the sun than a closed system (page 16)

4 identify containers made of insulated materials as ineffective in trapping solar energy (page 17).

Energy from the sun is called **solar energy**. The sun is a renewable energy source – it will not run out. Every day the sun supplies us with five hundred times more energy than we use. Solar energy has many advantages and it is free. Solar energy can be **converted** (changed) into heat energy which we can use.

Activity 1 Which is the best solar collector?

Your group will need:
- some styrofoam trays
- 4 clear plastic containers (diameter 7.5 cm)
- a pair of scissors
- aluminium foil 30 cm × 10 cm
- masking tape
- black paper 30 cm × 10 cm
- white paper 30 cm × 10 cm
- 4 thermometers
- clock or watch

1 Mark and cut out four styrofoam covers for the clear plastic containers (see diagram).

Safety!

- Do not punch the hole in the styrofoam lid with the thermometer. Use the pair of scissors or the point of a pencil.

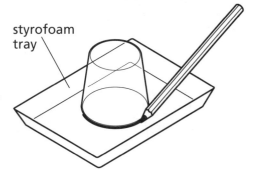

styrofoam tray

2 Wrap the aluminium foil around one container up to three-quarters of the height of the container. Allow a slight overlap. Mark the foil where it overlaps. Unwrap the foil and then cut it along the mark.

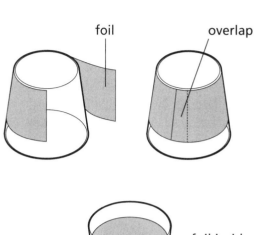

foil   overlap

3 Roll the foil to the shape of the container. Place the foil in the container.

4 Line the inside of the styrofoam lid with Place the foil in the container.

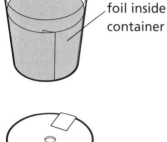

foil inside container

5 Punch a hole in the centre of the styrofoam lid. Tape the lid on the container.

6 Using white paper instead of foil repeat 2, 3, 4 and 5 for the second container.

7 Using black paper instead of foil repeat 2, 3, 4 and 5 and for the third container.

8 For the fourth container just punch a hole in the centre of the styrofoam lid and tape the lid to the container.

9 Put a thermometer into the hole of each lid. The thermometers must fit snugly into the holes. The thermometers must not touch the sides or the bottom of the containers.

10 Place the four containers next to each other, but not touching each other, in a sunny area.

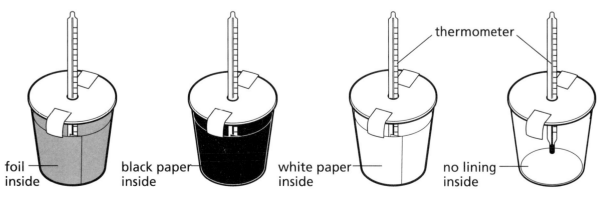

foil inside   black paper inside   white paper inside   thermometer   no lining inside

13

11 Record the starting temperature in each container. Record the temperature again every two minutes for the next 20 minutes in a table like Table 1.

Table 1

Time in minutes (up to 20)	Temperature in °C			
	foil	black	white	clear
0				
2				
4				
6 and so on				

12 Discuss questions **a)** to **d)** with your group. When you all agree, write the answers in your notebooks.

Help each other

a) What caused the temperature in the containers to change?

b) Which container had the highest temperature in the 20 minute period?
Can you explain why?

c) In which container was the lowest temperature recorded?
Can you explain why?

d) What colour would you paint a metal solar energy collector. Why?

When solar energy passes through glass or clear plastic, it is converted into heat energy. Materials like the lining in the plastic containers absorb heat energy. This makes the air in the containers get hotter. The increase in temperature depends on how much heat energy is absorbed. The container with the black lining absorbed the most heat energy so the temperature rose the most.

Solar energy in everyday life

Activity 1 suggests a possible method for collecting solar energy. This method can be used in two ways.

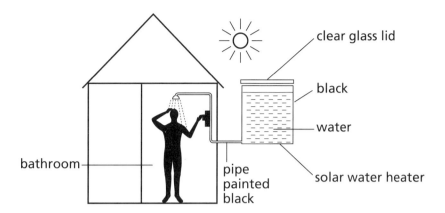

(1) The heat can be transferred (passed on) to water. For example, if you put water in a tank painted black, inside and outside, with a clear glass or plastic lid and let the sun shine on it, the water will heat up. The hot water can flow through pipes in a house and be used for washing and bathing (see the diagram above).

(2) Rooms in a building may be heated in the same way as the air in the containers was heated in Activity 1. Surfaces in the room absorb solar energy and heat up the air.

Many homes in Barbados are designed with solar collectors. Many houses have solar collectors on their roofs.

Explain how solar energy is used in this picture.

Discuss some advantages of using solar energy in the West Indies. When you all agree, write three advantages in your notebooks.

Project

In 1969 Professor Oliver Headley, a Chemistry lecturer at UWI, invented a solar energy system to collect clean (distilled) water for use in science classes. Professor Headley's system can be seen in secondary schools in Trinidad and Tobago. Visit a school and write a report on one system you observe.

Activity 2 Closed and open containers

Your group will need:
- the clear plastic container and lid lined with black paper from Activity 1
- another clear plastic container lined with black paper but without a complete lid
- piece of styrofoam
- masking tape
- 2 thermometers

Look at the safety note on page 12.

1 What do you think would have happened if you had left the lids of the plastic containers off in Activity 1? Write down your answer in your notebooks.

2 Discuss with your group a plan to test this out using the equipment listed. Discuss your plan with your teacher.

3 Now try out your plan.

4 Draw your apparatus as you set it up.

5 Prepare a table like Table 2 below and complete it.

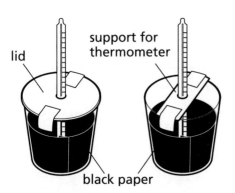

Table 2

Time in minutes (up to 20)	Temperature in °C	
	covered container	uncovered container
0		
2		
4		

6 Did the information in your table agree with your answer to 1 above? Sign your work and show your teacher.

7 Does an open container or a closed container absorb more solar energy?

Activity 3 A problem to solve

Carissa and Reagan believe that the shower in the diagram on page 15 would provide only cold water when the sun is covered by a cloud or at night. Reagan suggested that if the container was made of an **insulating** material, which prevents heat loss, the water in the container would keep hot for a long time. Styrofoam is a heat insulating material. But Carissa said that water in a styrofoam container would not get very hot. In your groups you are going to investigate whether Carissa is right.

Your group will need:
- a clear plastic container and lid from Activity 1 or 2
- a styrofoam cup (the same size as the plastic container) with a lid
- black paper
- 2 thermometers
- masking tape

1 Cover the *outside* of both the clear plastic container and the styrofoam cup (up to three-quarters of their height) and lids with black paper. Tape the black paper on.

2 Discuss a plan to test Carissa's statement. Tell your teacher.

3 Now go ahead with your plan.

4 Write down what you did. Draw up a table similar to Table 2 in Activity 2 and call it Table 3. Use it to record the temperatures in the clear plastic container and the styrofoam cup.

5 Draw the apparatus as you set it up.

6 Look at your observations in Table 3. Do you think Carissa is right?

7 All group members sign your work and show it to your teacher.

You should have found that the temperature of the water in the styrofoam cup increased very little. The temperature increased more in the plastic container. This is because an insulator like styrofoam can keep heat in but it is not good at absorbing heat from outside. So in order to have hot water at night or in cloudy weather we collect hot water in a solar collector which is made out of a material which aborbs a lot of heat. The water can then be pumped into an insulated tank and kept warm for some time.

Summary

- Energy from the sun is called solar energy. It can be converted into heat energy. In the activities, solar energy was changed to heat energy. The heat energy was trapped in the container. We made a solar energy collector.
- Water heated in a solar energy collector can be passed through pipes in a building to provide hot water for bathing and washing.
- Different materials absorb different amounts of heat energy. Black materials absorb heat energy best. Solar energy collectors are painted black.
- A solar heater cannot be made from an insulating material because the solar energy cannot pass through an insulating material as easily as through a non-insulating material.
- Solar energy provides clean, safe and reliable energy. The supply can not run out and it is inexpensive to use. However, solar energy is not available at night or during cloudy weather.

Test yourself ✏

For each task write down **A**, **B**, **C** or **D**.

1 Solar energy can be absorbed and transferred to water heating systems. A group of students painted four tins. They experimented with them to find the best colour to paint a solar collector. They used red, black, yellow and blue paint. The solar collector with the hottest water after one hour was the one painted

A red   **B** black   **C** yellow   **D** blue

(Objective 1)

2 The two containers X and Y in the diagram were left in the sun for two hours.

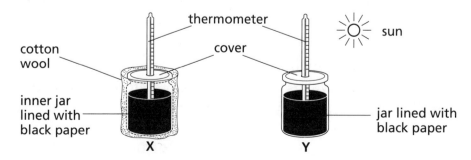

After the two hours the thermometer

A in X showed a higher temperature

B in Y showed a higher temperature

C in both systems showed the same increase in temperature

D in both systems showed no increase in temperature

(Objective 4)

3 X in the diagram has a lid. Y has no lid. They were both left in the sun. After two hours the thermometer

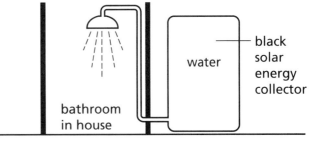

thermometer
lid   clear plastic   no lid
container
lined with
black paper
X   Y

A in both containers showed the same temperature increase

B in neither of the containers showed a temperature increase

C in X showed a greater increase in temperature

D in Y showed a greater increase in temperature

(Objective 3)

4 The people living in a house with a solar collector like the one in the diagram would get a hot shower

A at night

B on a cold rainy day

C on a cloudy day

D on a hot sunny day

Give a reason for your answer.

water   black solar energy collector

bathroom in house

(Objective 2)

5 Your task is to use the materials in the diagram to create a solar water purification system. With your system you must be able to get clean water from the muddy water in the large pan. Measure the depth of clean water you get in the jar every day for three days. Prepare a table to record your observations. Bring your solar water purification system to school and tell the other pupils how it works.

small jam jar

muddy water   masking tape   stone   plastic wrap

(Performance assessment)

Solutions

Objectives

At the end of the chapter pupils should be able to

1 identify which mixtures are suspensions and which can be fully dissolved (pages 20–22)

2 separate a mixture by the method of filtration (pages 22–24)

3 recover by the method of evaporation substances which had been dissolved in water (pages 24–25).

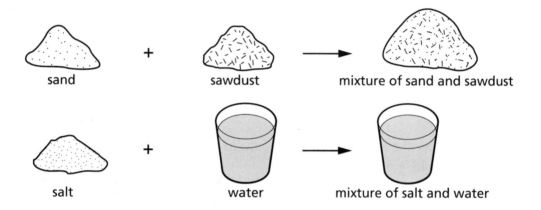

sand   +   sawdust   →   mixture of sand and sawdust

salt   +   water   →   mixture of salt and water

A **mixture** is made up of two or more substances. It can be a solid with a solid, like the sand and sawdust, or a solid and a liquid, as with the salt and water. The substances in a mixture can be separated. In this chapter we are going to look at mixtures of solids and liquids.

Activity 1 One type of mixture

Your group will need:
- 2 clear plastic containers
- a teaspoon
- sugar
- salt
- water

> Bring material to school when asked

1 Half fill one of the containers with water. Put two teaspoons of sugar in the water. Can you see the sugar?

2 Stir the sugar and water. Keep watching the sugar. Are the sugar particles getting smaller and smaller? Keep stirring. Can you see the sugar particles now? Does the water and the sugar all look the same?

3 Repeat steps **1** and **2** using salt instead of sugar. Did the salt particles get smaller and smaller until you could no longer see them? Does the mixture of salt and water look the same all the way through?

When a solid mixes with a liquid so that the mixture is the same all the way through a **solution** is formed.

In a solution the solid substance **dissolves** in the liquid so that it seems to disappear. The solid that dissolves is called the **solute**. The liquid that the solid dissolves in is called the **solvent**.

The solute breaks up into particles so small that they seem to disappear from our view into the solvent. They become invisible to the human eye, even with the aid of a microscope. Stirring the mixture helps the solute to dissolve more quickly in the liquid.

Activity 2 Another type of mixture

Your group will need:
- a teaspoon
- some sawdust
- some sand
- grated chalk
- water
- 4 clear plastic containers

Get into your groups quietly

1 Mix two teaspoons of sawdust in a container half-filled with water. Stir. Allow to stand.

2 Repeat step **1** using sand, then using grated chalk in separate containers.

3 Discuss **a)** to **e)** with your group. When you all agree write the answers in your notebook in the form of sentences.

   a) Did the particles of sawdust, sand and grated chalk get smaller and smaller as you stirred the mixture?

   b) Did the particles of sawdust, sand and grated chalk disappear from your sight?

   c) Did the mixtures appear to be the same all the way through?

   d) What happened to the mixtures after you allowed them to stand for some time?

   e) Were solutions formed with the sawdust and water, with the sand and water, and with the grated chalk and water?

The chalk, sand or sawdust did not break up into particles small enough to dissolve in the water. You could still see them. But the small particles were scattered right through the water. They were suspended in the water. We call a mixture like this a **suspension**.

Many suspensions separate when they are allowed to stand. The solid sinks to the bottom. You can often pour the upper layer off to separate the components of the mixture. This is called **decanting**. When one component is a solid you can separate it from the liquid by **filtering**.

salt + water

sand + water

Take turns to answer questions

solution

suspension

Activity 3 Separating a suspension

Your group will need:
- 2 clear plastic containers
- a funnel
- a filter paper (or blotting paper cut 12.5 cm in diameter)
- a tablespoon
- grated chalk or sand
- water
- a tin cover
- a large straw

Help each other

1 Put about 50 ml of water into one plastic container.

2 Put a tablespoon of grated chalk or sand into the container.

3 Stir the chalk–water (or sand–water) suspension with the straw. Leave to stand.

4 Fold the filter paper (or blotting paper) like this:

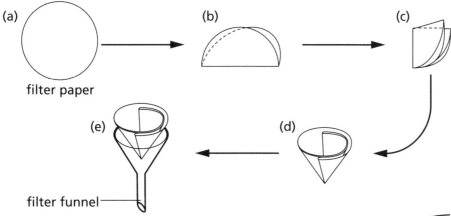

5 Wet the filter funnel. Fit the filter paper into the funnel. Fit the funnel into the top of the other container.

6 Pour the chalk–water (or sand–water) suspension on to the filter paper in the funnel. What passed through the filter paper?

7 Take the filter paper out of the funnel. What did you find in the filter paper? Empty it into a tin cover.

8 Leave it to dry (the water will evaporate).

9 Discuss these two questions with your group. Write your answers in your notebooks.

Talk quietly

a) Does chalk/sand dissolve?

b) How did you remove the water from the chalk/sand?

Observing

In Activity 3 you separated the chalk or sand from the water by **filtration**. We can separate a suspension by this method. What is left in the filter paper is called the **residue**. In this activity the chalk and the sand were the residues. The water passed through the filter paper. We call the substance which passes through the filter paper the **filtrate**.

Activity 4 Recovering the solute from a solution

Your group will need:
- 2 clear plastic containers
- a funnel
- filter paper (or blotting paper as before)
- a teaspoon
- a metal tablespoon
- 2 tablespoons of salt
- 150 ml water
- a large straw
- a hand lens
- a candle
- a tray with sand in which to place the candle

Safety!
- Only your teacher should light the candle and heat the mixture over the flame. Keep the candle in the sand tray. Stand at a safe distance.

1 Put 50 ml of water into a plastic container. Add a tablespoon of salt.

2 Stir the mixture until all the salt dissolves.

3 Fold the filter paper (or blotting paper) as in the diagram in Activity 3.

4 Wet the funnel and fit the filter paper in place. Put a plastic container under the funnel.

5 Pour the salt solution on to the filter paper in the funnel.

6 Remove the filter paper. Is there any residue? What do you think this is?

7 Put the used filter paper into the waste bin.

Note: the next part must be done by your teacher.

8 Your teacher will light your candle in the sand tray.

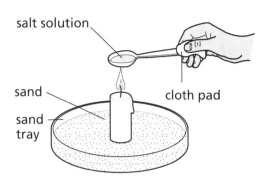

salt solution

sand

sand tray

cloth pad

9 Put some of the liquid from the plastic container into an old metal spoon. Your teacher will hold the spoon carefully over the lighted candle. Watch as the water evaporates from the salt solution.

10 Discuss the following questions with your group. When you all agree, write a sentence to answer each question in your notebooks.

a) Why did you stir the salt and water?

b) Why did the salt solution pass through the filter paper?

c) Does salt dissolve?

d) How did you get the salt back from the salt solution?

e) Where did the water go?

f) Could the solvent evaporate without using the heat from a candle?

You **recovered** the salt from the solution by **evaporation**. When you heated the salt solution the water evaporated away from the solution. The salt was left behind.

What was left on the filter paper may be undissolved salt or bits of dirt. The salt which dissolved passed through the filter paper. Therefore, you could not separate the salt from the water by filtration.

Summary

* A mixture consists of two or more substances mixed together. The substances can be separated. They are components of the mixture.
* A solution is a mixture in which the solute breaks down into tiny particles and mixes evenly with the solvent, e.g. salt and water.
* A suspension is a mixture in which particles of one substance remain scattered through another substance without dissolving, e.g. sand and water.
* A suspension can be separated into its components by filtration.
* The components of a solution cannot be separated by filtration. The solute can be recovered by evaporation of the solvent.

Test yourself ✏

For each task write down **A**, **B**, **C** or **D**.

1 In a true solution, a solute dissolves in the

    A residue   **B** mixture

    C filtrate   **D** solvent

(Objective 1)

2 Harry had a clear liquid that was a mixture. He boiled away the liquid. A solid remained. The liquid and the solid made up

    A a solution

    B a filtration

    C neither solution nor filtration

    D a residue

(Objective 1)

3 A group made two mixtures and left them to settle.

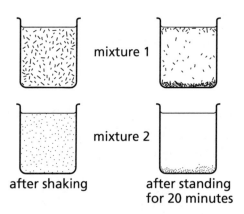

mixture 1

mixture 2

after shaking   after standing for 20 minutes

From looking at the diagram, you can deduce that

    A Mixture 1 is a solution

    B Mixture 2 is a solution

    C Neither mixture 1 nor 2 is a solution

    D Both mixtures 1 and 2 are solutions

Give a reason for your choice.

(Objective 1)

Use these diagrams to answer questions 4 and 5.

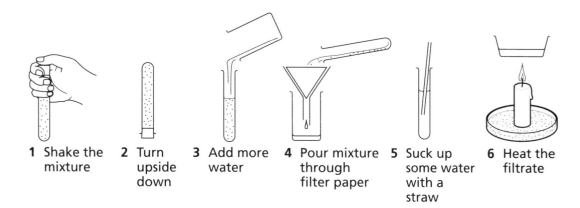

1 Shake the mixture 2 Turn upside down 3 Add more water 4 Pour mixture through filter paper 5 Suck up some water with a straw 6 Heat the filtrate

4 If you wanted to recover the solute from a solution, which two tasks would you perform?

   A 1 and 3   **B** 3 and 5

   C 2 and 5   **D** 4 and 6

(Objective 2)

5 Which diagram shows separating the filtrate and the residue?

   A 4 only   **B** 2 and 5 only

   C 6 only   **D** 3 and 5 only

   Give a reason for your choice.

(Objective 3)

6 Collect some white sand and mix it with salt. Set up an experiment to separate the sand from the salt. Draw the apparatus you used and explain how you used it.

(Performance assessment)

7 Find how many paperclips will balance a teaspoon of salt.
   Dissolve the teaspoon of salt in water. Recover the salt.
   Find the mass of the salt you have recovered.
   State whether any solid material is lost when you evaporate a solution.
   Write a report on what you did.

(Performance assessment)

Is Air Matter?

> ## Objectives
>
> At the end of the chapter pupils should be able to
> 1 show air occupies space (pages 28–29)
> 2 show air has mass (pages 30–31).

All matter has mass and takes up space. We can't see air but air is all around us. Does it take up any space? Does it have mass?

Activity 1 Does air occupy space?

Your group will need:
- a 473 ml soft drink bottle (cut to make it 8 cm tall)
- a bottle cap
- a clear plastic container
- a plastic bucket
- a large ice-cream tub

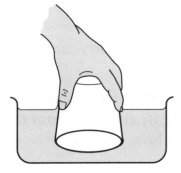

> Bring materials to class when asked

1 Fill the ice-cream tub almost to the top with water.

2 Push the clear plastic container straight down in the water open end down. Did the water fill up the container?

3 Screw the bottle cap onto the bottle.

4 Fill the plastic bucket three-quarters full with water.

5 Push the bottle straight down into the water, open end down (see diagram). Did the water fill up the bottle?

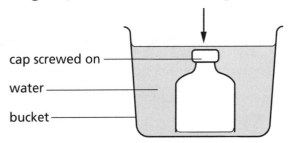

cap screwed on

water

bucket

6 Unscrew the top just a little while the bottle is still under the water. Discuss what you observe with your group.

7 Discuss what happened with your group. Why do you think water did not enter the container and the bottle in steps 2 and 5? Why do you think the water entered the bottle in step 6?

Activity 2 Fill it up if you can

Your group will need:

- a 473 ml clean soft drink bottle (with a hole punched in it near the neck)
- a funnel
- plasticine
- a clear plastic container
- an ice pick

Help each other

Safety!

- Only your teacher will use the ice pick to make the hole in the soft drink bottle.

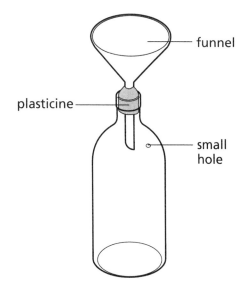

1 Fit the funnel into the bottle and plug around the stem with plasticine (see the diagram).

2 Fill the plastic container with water.

3 Put your finger on the hole at the side of the bottle. Another person briskly pours the water into the funnel. Observe what happens to the water.

4 When the funnel is filled with water, take your finger away. Observe what happens to the water.

5 Discuss with your group why the water did not fall into the bottle at step 3 and why it did in step 4.

6 Does air occupy space?

Activity 3 Does air have mass?

Your group will need:
- 5 balloons of the same size and type
- a metre rule
- thread (about 40 cm long)
- a pin
- string (about 20 cm long)
- tape
- a balance (optional)

1 Tie the piece of string to the centre of the metre stick. Hold the end of the string. Is the stick level? Move the string on the stick until the stick hangs level. When the stick balances, tape the string in place to secure it.

2 Blow up two balloons by blowing 20 times into each. Knot the necks of the balloons. Tie a piece of thread round the end of each balloon.

3 Tie a balloon to each end of the metre stick.

4 When the balloons balance, put a piece of tape on the thread of each to keep them steady (see diagram).

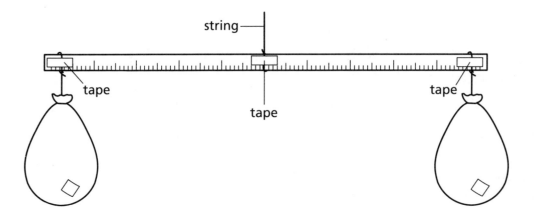

5 Burst one of the balloons with a pin.

6 Discuss what you observed with your group.

7 Why did the balloons no longer balance when you burst one of them? Write down your explanation in your notebooks.

If you have a balance continue with steps 8 to 12.

8 Find the mass of four uninflated balloons.

9 Calculate the mass of one uninflated balloon.

10 Inflate one balloon by blowing 20 times into it. Find the mass.

11 Calculate the mass of the air you put into the inflated balloon (with 20 blows).

12 Does air have mass? Is air matter?

Summary

- Air takes up space. A glass standing on a table is filled with air. A glass held upside down is filled with air.
- If a bottle or a glass is filled with air, water cannot fill up the bottle or glass unless the air is removed because air occupies space.
- Two balloons of the same size will balance each other if there is the same volume of air in each. If we let the air out of one of the balloons they will no longer balance. Therefore air has mass.
- Air has mass and takes up space. So air is matter.

Test yourself ✏

For each task write down **A**, **B**, **C** or **D**.

1 Quilan hit the top of the box with a sharp slap. The lighted candle went out because

A air from Quilan's hand blew the flame out

B air in the box was forced through the hole and blew out the candle

C there was a sudden strong breeze coming from outside

D the teacher blew out the candle

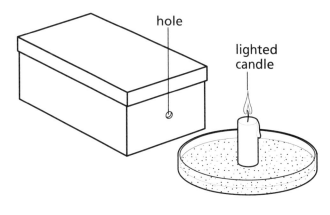

(Objective 1)

2 Ryan pushed a container with a paper towel in the bottom straight down into the water open end down. When Ryan took out the container, the paper towel was dry because

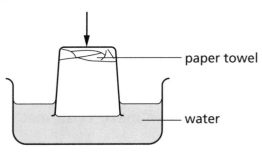

A a paper towel dries quickly

B there was grease on the container

C Ryan pushed down the container slowly

D the container remained filled with air

(Objective 1)

3 Anna pushed a test tube straight down into a beaker of water. Little water entered the tube. She attached a tube to a syringe and pushed the tube into the almost empty test tube. Anna pulled the plunger out and found that

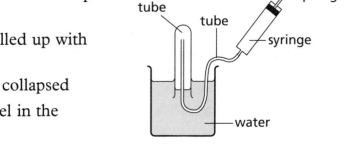

A the water almost filled up the test tube

B the syringe filled up with water

C the test tube collapsed

D the water level in the beaker rose

Explain why you chose that answer.

(Objective 1)

4 Heddi and Zack experimented to find out if air occupied space. They used their apparatus as in the diagram. The experiment that demonstrated that air occupies space was

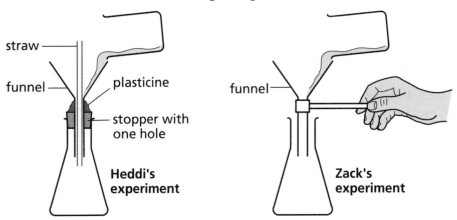

A Heddi's only

B Zack's only

C neither Heddi's nor Zack's

D both Heddi's and Zack's

Explain why you chose that answer.

(Objective 1)

5 Nicky and Raphael each set up an experiment to find out if air has mass. They used the same size balloon in each case. The experiment that demonstrated that air has mass is

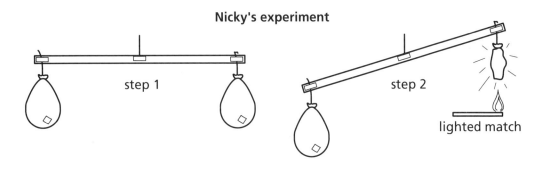

Nicky's experiment

step 1

step 2

lighted match

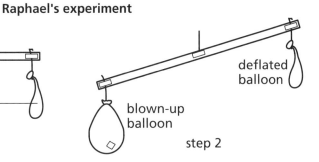

Raphael's experiment

deflated balloons

step 1

deflated balloon

blown-up balloon

step 2

A Nicky's only

B Raphael's only

C neither Nicky's nor Raphael's

D both Nicky's and Raphael's

Explain why you chose that answer.

(Objective 2)

Gears

> ## Objectives
>
> At the end of the chapter pupils should be able to
>
> 1 identify which way gears move when you operate them
>   (pages 34–35)
>
> 2 identify a gear-wheel that causes another gear-wheel to move faster,
>   slower or at the same speed (pages 35–36)
>
> 3 show the input gear and the output gear in a system of gears
>   (page 35)
>
> 4 identify and name machines that use gears (page 36).

Can you think of some machines at home or at school that use gears?
This chapter will help you to find out what gears do and how they can
go faster or slower, and change the direction things move in.

Activity 1 Turn, turn, turn

Your group will need:
- **1 small gear-wheel with 10 teeth (see the Teacher's Guide)**
- **1 large gear-wheel with 20 teeth**

1 Turn the larger gear-wheel against the
   smaller gear-wheel.

2 Does the smaller gear-wheel turn in the
   same direction as the large gear-wheel?

3 Does the smaller gear-wheel move at
   the same speed as the large
   gear-wheel?

4 Turn the larger gear-wheel right round
   once.
   How many times does the smaller gear-wheel turn right round?

5 Now turn the smaller gear-wheel four times. How many times does
   the larger gear-wheel turn?

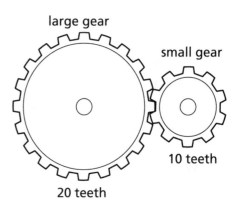

large gear

small gear

10 teeth

20 teeth

The gear-wheel which you turn is called the **input gear**. When you turned the larger gear, the larger gear was the input gear. When you turned the smaller gear, that was the input gear. The gear turned by the input gear is called the **output gear**. In the first part of the activity the output gear was the smaller gear, in the second part of the activity, it was the larger gear. The input gear makes the output gear turn.

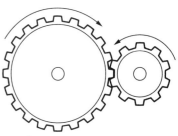

input gear   output gear

Did you notice that the output gear turns in the opposite direction to the input gear? You can use gears to change the direction of movement.

Activity 2   A rule about gears

Your group will need:
- **2 gear-wheels with 10 teeth**
- **1 gear-wheel with 5 teeth**
- **1 board with 3 short dowels**

1 Put the two gear-wheels with 10 teeth, A and A_1, over two dowels.

2 Turn gear A in a clockwise direction (see arrow in diagram).

3 In what direction does the other gear A_1 turn?

4 Do both gears turn at the same speed?

5 Remove gear A_1. Put on gear B.

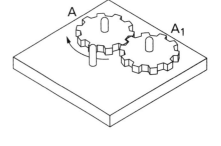

6 Discuss with your group which gear would move faster if you turned gear A (the input gear) anti-clockwise as shown in the diagram. In what direction would B (the output gear) turn?

7 Now turn gear A (the input gear) to see whether your prediction was correct.

8 Suppose you replace gear B with gear C and gear C is bigger than gear A. Would C turn slower or faster than B? Draw the gears to show how they would work.

When gears A and B are turned, B will go around twice as many times as A does. There is a simple rule that can give you this answer without turning the gears. Discuss what this rule might be with your group. When you all agree, write the answer down in your notebooks.

Watches, clocks, the gearbox of a motorcar, the egg beater, the hand drill, the wrench and some toys all use gears.

Summary
- A gear-wheel is a wheel with teeth.
- When one gear-wheel turns another gear-wheel it can pass on turning motion. The motion is in the opposite direction.
- Gears may produce speed changes in machines. The speed changes when gears of different sizes connect. The smaller gear always turns faster than the larger one. The number of teeth in the gears can tell you how many times faster the small gear will turn than the larger gear. If the larger gear has 30 teeth and the smaller gear has 10 teeth, the smaller gear will turn 3 times as fast as the larger gear.
- When two gears have the same number of teeth they move at the same speed. Such a system is usually used to change the direction of motion.
- The gear that you apply a force to is called the input gear. The input gear passes on force and energy to the output gear.

Test yourself

For each task write down **A**, **B**, **C** or **D** and give a reason for your answer. The diagram below should be used for Tasks 1 and 2.

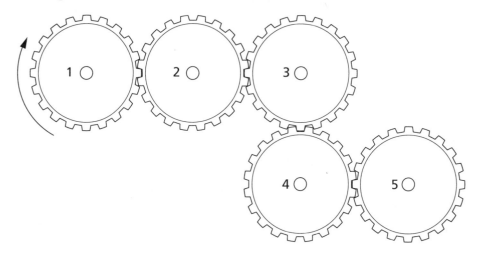

1 When Kerry turns gear 1 clockwise, gear 4 will turn

   A in the same direction as 3

   B in the opposite direction to 2

   C in the opposite direction to 1

   D in the same direction as 5

(Objective 1)

2 When Baksh turns gear 1 in a clockwise direction, gear 5 turns in

   A the same direction and faster than 1

   B an opposite direction and slower than 1

   C an opposite direction and the same speed as 1

   D the same direction and the same speed as 1

(Objectives 1 and 2)

3 In the diagram below there are two gears. The input gear will

   A move slower than the output gear

   B move faster than the output gear

   C move at the same speed as the output gear

   D not move the output gear

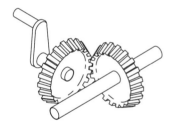

(Objective 2)

4 Gears 1 and 4 in the diagram are the same size. Gears 2 and 3 are the same size. In the diagram gear 4 is

   A the output gear

   B the input gear

   C both the input and output gear

   D neither the input nor the output gear

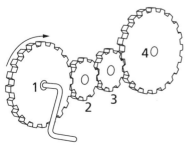

(Objective 3)

5 In the hand drill in the diagram

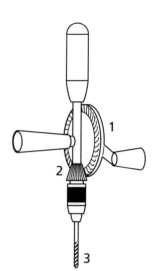

A 1 is the input gear

B 2 is the input gear

C 1 is the output gear

D 3 is the input gear

(Objective 3)

6 Which of the following has a gear system?
   A the fan belt in a car
   B a gear stick knob
   C an egg beater
   D a pulley with a large and a small wheel

(Objective 4)

7 Assemble a gear system to make a gear *lock*. That is, when you turn the handle there is no movement.

   a) Make a drawing of the system you propose to make.

   b) Try the system that you drew. If it does not work, try again.

   c) Make a final drawing of the working system.

(Performance assessment)

Surface Tension

Objectives

At the end of the chapter pupils should be able to

1 demonstrate surface tension by floating objects in water which normally sink (pages 39–40)

2 identify and describe the effect of soap on surface tension as water rises above the top of a glass (pages 40–41)

3 demonstrate and describe the effect of soap on surface tension (page 41)

4 identify and describe the effect of soap on the movement of water into paper and cloth (pages 41–42)

5 identify and describe the effect of soap (or detergent) on washing out dirt from clothes (pages 42–43).

Activity 1   Overfilled not overflowed

Your group will need:
- a clear plastic container
- 80 1¢ coins
- a dropper
- a hand lens
- a clear canister with a teaspoon of liquid soap or detergent

Safety!
- Wash your hands after the activity.

1 Fill the plastic container with water so that the water surface is level with the top of the container.

2 Discuss with your group how many 1¢ coins you think you could put into the container of water before it overflows. Write down your prediction.

3 Carefully put one coin at a time sideways, not flat, into the water.

4 Keep adding the coins and counting them. Keep looking at the surface of the water as you add the coins.

5 After you have added about 50 or 60 coins, draw the container. Show what the top of the water looks like.

6 Keep adding coins until the water overflows. How many coins have you added? Was your prediction very good, good, or not so good?

7 Add two or three drops of liquid soap to the water in the container. What happened?

8 Discuss with your group what you think happened to the water surface when you added the liquid soap. When you all agree, write down your answer in your notebook.

At the surface of the water, the particles of water are strongly pulled together. This makes the surface of water behave as if it was covered by an invisible skin that holds it in. This is called **surface tension**.

Surface tension allows water to bulge over the top of a container without spilling. When the liquid soap falls on to the water it breaks the links between the particles of water and therefore causes the water to overflow.

Activity 2 A floating sinker

Your group will need:
- a dropper
- 2 paperclips about 3 cm long
- a hand lens
- a clear plastic container
- liquid soap

> All problems are to be solved by the group

1 Do you think a paperclip can float? Fill the container about three-quarters full with water. Drop one of your paperclips into the container. What happened?

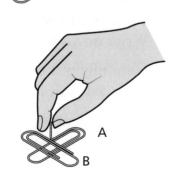

paperclip A

2 Take the paperclip out of the water.

3 Shape one of the paperclips (A) as shown in the diagram.

4 Rest the other paperclip B on paperclip A. Hold clip A at X.

5 Lower the clips into the container slowly and carefully.

6 Let paperclip B rest on the surface of the water.

7 Take paperclip A away without disturbing paperclip B. Does the paperclip float?

8 Look carefully at paperclip B and the surface of the water around it. (Use your hand lens.)

9 Discuss with your group what you observe about the paperclip and the water surface around it. Leave the paperclip floating.

10 Discuss with your group why the paperclip floated when you placed it gently on the water, but sank when you dropped it into the water. Write your explanation in your notebooks.

11 Discuss with your group what you think would happen if you placed a drop of liquid soap on the surface of the water. When you all agree, write down your prediction in your notebook.

12 Now add a drop of soap to the surface of the water near to the floating paperclip. Were you right?

13 Sign your work and show your teacher.

> Help each other contribute ideas

Activity 3 Sink or swim

Your group will need:
- a piece of newspaper or cloth (12 cm × 6 cm)
- a pair of scissors
- a metric ruler
- 2 clear plastic containers
- liquid soap
- a dropper

1 Fold the piece of newspaper in half. Draw a paper doll. Cut out and get two similar dolls.

2 Add water to three-quarters fill up each clear plastic container.

3 In one container, put 15 drops of liquid soap. Stir gently.

Safety!
- Do not play with the scissors.

tap water   soapy water

4 Hold a paper doll upright over each container. Drop them straight down into the containers together.

5 What happened to the doll that you dropped into the soapy water? What happened to the doll that you dropped into the tap water? Discuss with your group why one doll became soaked more quickly than the other. Will the same thing happen with cloth dolls? Try it.

Soap breaks some of the links between the water particles at the water surface. This reduces surface tension (it weakens the water 'skin'). So water can soak into the paper more quickly. Why did one doll sink before the other?

Activity 4 Why we need soap

Your group will need:
- a piece of old dry cloth about the size of a handkerchief
- some dirt in a tin cover
- a teaspoon of grease in a tin cover
- some liquid soap (3 teaspoonfuls)
- 3 butter tubs each with water
- newspaper

Safety!
- Wash your hands after the activity.

1 Cut the cloth into three equal pieces. Mark them A, B and C.

2 Rub a little dirt spot on to a corner of each piece of cloth.

3 Wash cloth A with water only. Did the dirt wash out?

4 Mix some grease with the dirt. Rub it on to cloth B and C.

5 Wash cloth B with water only. Did the dirt and grease wash out?

6 Add some liquid soap to the dirt-grease spot on cloth C and rub it in. Now wash cloth C with water. Did the dirt and the grease wash out?

7 Discuss 5 above with your group. Why do you think the water did not wash out the dirt and grease? Write down your group's ideas in your notebook.

How soap removes grease

A soap particle

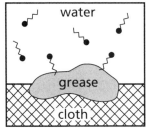

Grease spot is 'attacked'

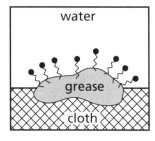

The grease-loving tails of the soap attach to the grease

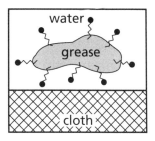

The grease is removed and washed away

water-loving head

grease-loving tail

Water slides along oil or grease. It cannot hold on to it to remove it from your hands or clothes. However, the particles of soap can latch themselves on to both oil and water. One end of the soap particle (the 'tail') sticks to grease particles. The other end (the 'head') sticks to water particles. The extra water can then wash the 'attached' water and dirty oil away.

Oil on your clothes comes from your body. Your skin gives off oil all the time. Dirt gets on your clothes and mixes with oil from your skin. Soap is needed to remove the dirt and oil.

Summary
- Some things which usually sink in water can float on the surface of the water. This is possible because strong forces seem to hold particles of water (and other liquids) together to form a kind of 'skin' on the top of the water. This is what is called surface tension.
- The surface tension allows water to bulge over the top of a glass when we overfill it with water.
- The links that hold the particles of water together are easily broken by soap and therefore soap breaks the surface tension.
- Water does not usually mix with oil or grease. Soap particles can stick on to both the oil and water. Extra water can then wash away the soap. This is why we need soap to wash off grease and oil.

Observing

Test yourself

For each task write down **A**, **B**, **C** or **D**.

1 The children kept adding water to a full glass of water. The water surface came up over the rim of the glass. This happened because

    A water surfaces are convex   **B** of surface tension

    C soap holds on to water and oil   **D** the children were very skilful

                      (Objective 2)

2 Two similar pieces of cloth were dropped into the two containers of water X and Y. X contained tap water. Y contained soapy water.

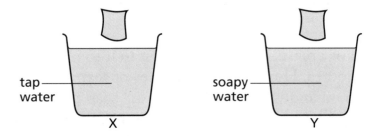

    A The cloth in X quickly absorbed water and sank

    B The cloth in Y quickly absorbed water and sank

    C Both pieces of cloth quickly absorbed water and sank

    D Neither piece of cloth absorbed water quickly

                      (Objective 4)

3 Mary had a needle floating on water. One way to make the needle sink without touching it would be to

    A leave it for ten seconds

    B put a drop of soap in the water

    C hold a weak magnet 1 centimetre from the needle

    D add some black pepper to the water

                      (Objective 3)

4 We use soap to remove dirt and grease from clothes because soap

    A is cheap

    B is slimy and causes dirt and grease to slip out of the clothes

    C latches on to both grease and water

    D makes clothes whiter

                      (Objective 5)

5 Lula carefully placed a razor blade on the surface of a dish of water. Jai dropped a needle into a dish of water point first. Jai's needle sank because

    A the needle is heavier than the razor blade

    B the surface tension at the point of the needle was too small

    C soap got on the needle by mistake

    D a needle can never, never float on water

(Objective 1)

6 Heddy put some talcum powder in a dish of water. The talcum power floated on the surface.

Harry put a drop of soap in the middle of the talcum powder. The talcum powder

    A dissolved in the water

    B spread out away from the soap drop

    C surrounded the soap drop closely

    D sank to the bottom immediately

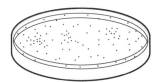

(Objective 3)

7 Two pupils each put 65 drops of water into a full glass of water. The water curved over the brim. One pupil added one drop of liquid soap to the water. The water immediately fell over the brim of the glass. The other pupil added one drop of water to his glass, nothing happened. The drop of soap

    A added volume to the already full glass of water

    B caused water to slip over the edge of the glass

    C made the water heavier

    D weakened the surface tension of the water

(Objective 2)

8 Cut out a boat like the one in the diagram from a piece of styrofoam tray $4 \, cm \times 2.5 \, cm$.

Float your boat in a styrofoam tray $21 \, cm \times 16 \, cm$ filled with clean tap water. Carefully put one drop of detergent (use a dropper) into the round hole at the back of the boat. Write a report on what you observe. Give an explanation of what happened.

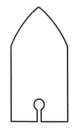

(Performance assessment)

Hard and Soft Water

Objectives

At the end of the chapter pupils should be able to

1 identify samples of water as hard or soft by their ability to form lather with soap (page 46)

2 classify samples of water as soft or hard by their ability to form lather with soap (pages 47–48).

Activity 1   Hard water test

Your group will need:
- **2 clear plastic soft drink bottles with caps**
- **a dropper**
- **a canister**
- **300 ml rainwater**
- **soap solution**
- **watch**

> Bring materials to class when asked

1 Fill one bottle half-full with rainwater and label it A.

2 Fill the other bottle half-full with the water to be tested. Label it B. The amount of water in A and B must be equal.

3 Get some soap solution from your teacher.

4 Put one drop of soap solution at a time in bottle A. After adding each drop shake the bottle vigorously 15 times. Put the bottle on its side. Wait until the **lather** (suds) begins to disappear. How long did it take?

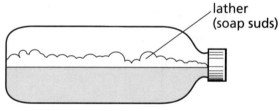

lather (soap suds)

5 Keep on adding soap solution. Stop when enough lather is formed to cover the surface of the water for one whole minute when the bottle is put on its side.

6 Record the number of drops you used.

7 Add the same number of drops of soap solution to the water you are testing in bottle B. If it produced the same amount of lather as in bottle A, the water is soft.

8 If you do not get enough lather, add more soap solution until you get the same amount of lather that the rainwater test produced. If you have to add a lot more soap, the water in B is hard water.

Rainwater is **soft water**. Soft water lathers easily with soap.
Hard water does not lather easily with soap.

Activity 2 How soft, how hard?

Your group will need:

- soap solution as in Activity 1
- 4 Cheers cylinders, each with a line marked 4 cm from the bottom (10 ml)
- sea water (salt water), rainwater, river water and pond water
- dropper
- 1 tablespoon
- ruler
- watch

> Sign your group report

1 Label your Cheers cylinders A, B, C and D.

2 Your teacher will give you four water samples. Put the sea water in cylinder A, rainwater in B, river water in C and pond water in D. Fill each cylinder to the 10 ml mark.

3 Put 4 drops of soap solution into cylinder A.

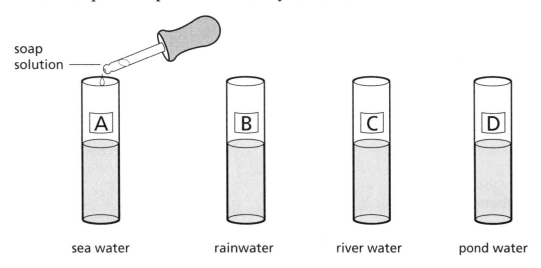

soap solution

sea water   rainwater   river water   pond water

4 Shake cylinder A vigorously ten times. Place the cylinder on your desk. Measure the height of the lather immediately.

5 Leave it to stand for ten minutes, then measure the height of the lather again.

6 Record your results in a table similar to Table 1 on the next page.

Table 1 *Height of lather in water samples*

	Height of lather			
	A	B	C	D
When we stopped shaking				
After 10 minutes				

7 Do the same as you did with sample A in steps 3 to 6 with the other water samples.

8 Which sample made the most lather? Which sample made the least amount of lather? Place the water samples in the order of hardness starting with the least hard.

9 Do you think the source of water has any effect on the amount of lather produced? Has it any effect on the hardness or softness of the water?

We use less soap to wash when we use soft water. In the activity, you had to use extra soap solution to get a good lather with the hard water. This represents the amount of soap wasted each time that hard water is used for washing. Some types of hard water can become soft water if you boil the water. Washing soda can make all types of hard water soft. People make bath salts by colouring and adding perfumes to washing soda.

Summary
- You can find out whether water is hard or soft by testing how quickly it forms a lather with soap, how much lather is created and how long the lather lasts. If a lather is formed quickly, there is a lot of lather and the lather remains for some time, then the water is soft. Rainwater and distilled water are soft.
- Some kinds of water do not form a lather readily with soap. This water is called hard water. Tap water and sea water are hard water.
- Some types of hard water become soft if you boil the water. Adding washing soda makes all hard water soft.
- When washing you use less soap if you use soft water (rainwater, or tap water with washing soda added) than when you use hard water. It is therefore cheaper to wash with soft water.

Test yourself

For each task write down **A**, **B**, **C** or **D**.

The table shows data recorded when pupils tested water samples with a soap solution. Use the data for tasks 1 and 2.

Water samples (100 ml in each container)	Volume of soap solution that gave a lather which remained for more than 10 minutes (in ml)
X	19
Y	3
Z	1

1 Rainwater was in

    A Y only   **B** Z only   **C** Y and Z only   **D** X only

                                                                     (Objective 1)

2 Tap water was in

    A X and Y only   **B** Z only   **C** Y only   **D** X only

                                                                     (Objective 1)

3 Someone boiled 100 ml of hard water. When the water was tested very little lather was formed with soap. The boiled water was

    A still hard water   **B** soft water

    C hard water sometimes and   **D** changed to another substance
       soft water sometimes

                                                                      (Objective 1)

4 Three samples of water X, Y and Z were tested with a soap solution. The results were as follows:
X made lather easily, Y made a lather easily only after boiling. Z did not make a lather easily after boiling. The classification for the three water samples is shown as:

	Soft water	Hard water
A	X,Y	Z
B	Y, Z	X
C	Y	X, Z
D	X	Y, Z

                                                                     (Objective 2)

5 Important qualities of soap are how quickly it lathers (makes suds), how much lather it makes and how long the lather lasts. Lather helps to spread the soap so more of the soap particles can work on greasy dirt. Select three detergents and perform a suitable experiment to find out which makes the most lather for the longest time.
Prepare a data table to show the height of the bubbles

a) when you stopped shaking
b) after 10 minutes
c) after 1 hour.

(Performance assessment)

Project Clean-up

Objectives

At the end of the chapter pupils should be able to

1 identify and classify items of litter around the school yard as recyclable, re-usable, non-recyclable, non-re-usable (pages 51–52)

2 set up a collection system for litter under the headings recyclable, re-usable, non-recyclable and non-re-usable (pages 52–53).

What can we do with litter?

When you drink a bottle of soda, you throw away the bottle. When something is used up, or we don't need it any more, we call it waste or litter and thrown it away. Waste can be unsightly and can be a health hazard. We can also waste natural resources by throwing things away.

Over the years, it has become more and more difficult to get rid of litter by burning and land-filling. Burning litter pollutes the atmosphere. We can't go on dumping rubbish in holes in the ground (land-filling areas) for ever. We must try to reduce the amount of litter we produce.

If we can find another use for the litter we call it a 're-usable' item. **Re-usable** items are things that you can keep on using if you repair or modify them, or that you can find new uses for.

Recycling means collecting things and reprocessing the materials they are made of. The materials can then be used to make something new. For example, glass bottles can be recycled to make new glass bottles.

Activity 1 Studying litter around your school

1 During break walk around your school yard and make a note of the litter you find.

2 List the types of litter that you find under the headings: glass, paper, food waste, metal, rubber, plastic and wood.

3 Discuss with your group whether you can re-use any of the items that you found. Say how you think they could be used. Discuss whether you can recycle any of the items you found. Enter the items in a table like Table 1 below.

Table 1

Item found	Re-usable	Use	Recylable	Non-recylable
Glass bottle	✓	as	✓	

We need to encourage people to re-use items because it saves throwing these items away and filling up land-fill sites.

Recycling old material saves in the use of raw materials when making new items, as in the case of glass.

Activity 2 A collection system

Safety!

• Lead is poisonous. Let an adult handle it.

1 Discuss with your group the classification of litter items in Table 1 of Activity 1. Now think about how you would collect the items for re-using, recycling and throwing away. Then copy Table 2 on the next page in your notebooks.

2 Discuss with your group why it is necessary to sort the recyclable items. When you all agree, write down why metal, paper, glass and plastics need to be sorted. For example, if green, brown and clear glass scraps were all melted together it would be impossible to make clear glass. Plastic bottles have symbols on them to show how they need to be separated (two of these symbols are given in the table – draw any others that you have seen). Think how paper might be separated out. Now complete Table 2. Some of the table has been filled out to help you. Add pictures of suitable containers for collecting the various items.

Table 2 *Collection methods*

Item groups	Separation method	Re-usable	Non-re-usable	Recyclable	Non-recylable
Metals	attracted by a magnet not attracted by a magnet	iron/steel aluminium	school bin	iron/steel aluminium lead	school bin
Paper	low grade ————				
Plastics	1 2				
Glass	green ———— ————	Returnable School or home use		G B C	

Summary

- Re-using and recycling are important ways of reducing litter and at the same time saving lots of money.
- We re-use things when we repair or alter them so we can go on using them, or find new uses for them.
- We recycle materials by processing them and using them to make new things.
- It is convenient to sort items that we re-use and recycle.
  1 Metals need to be classified as iron, aluminium and lead.
  2 Paper needs to be classified as low grade and high grade.
  3 Glass is classified according to its colour.
  4 Plastics are classified according to the type of plastic. Symbols with numbers indicate the type of plastic.

Test yourself

For each task write down **A, B, C** or **D**.

1 Mary is re-using when she gives which items to a school library?

  A journals and beer bottles   **B** magazines and plastic bottles

  C magazines and journals   **D** aluminium tins and copybooks

(Objective 1)

2 Which of the following can be re-used to make an aquarium?

  A an old ball-point pen

  B a 2 litre clear plastic bottle

  C aluminium soft drink cans

  D a pair of shoes that have become too small for the owner

(Objective 1)

3 Which of the following items is recycled?

  A scrap newspaper reduced to pulp and made into paper bags

  B notebook pages used to write on a clean side

  C clothes that you have outgrown and give to someone else

  D a large bottle made into a bedside lamp

(Objective 1)

4 Litter items that are classified according to colour are

  A plastics   **B** metals

  C paper   **D** glass

(Objective 2)

5 The symbol ⟨2⟩ is found on items made of

  A plastic   **B** metal

  C paper   **D** glass

(Objective 2)

Plant Life

Objectives

At the end of the chapter pupils should be able to

1 describe changes which take place in a seedling that is placed in a dark box with light entering through a hole (pages 55–56)

2 demonstrate and describe the effect of the presence or absence of water on seeds (pages 57–58)

3 state differences observed in seedlings watered twice per day and others watered twice per week (pages 58–59).

Activity 1 Let there be light

Your group will need:
- a shoebox painted black inside, or with black paper covering the inside
- lentil seedlings
- 1 styrofoam cup cut 4 cm tall
- cotton wool

1 Make a hole 1 cm diameter at one end of the shoebox, 4 cm from the bottom.

2 Your teacher will give you 4 or 5 seedlings like the one in the diagram.

3 Put 4 seedlings on some cotton wool in the styrofoam cup.

4 Place the cup in the shoebox 2.5 cm from the hole. Cover the box.

> **Bring materials to class when asked**

Safety!
- Wash your hands after this activity.

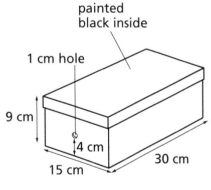

painted black inside

1 cm hole

9 cm

4 cm

15 cm

30 cm

lentil seedling

Communicating

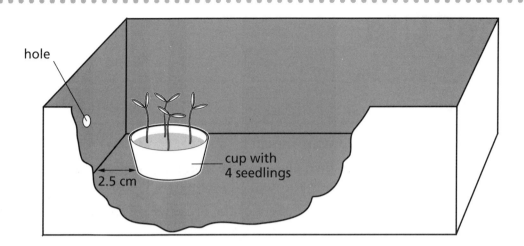

hole

2.5 cm

cup with
4 seedlings

5 Put the box near a window with the hole facing the light.

6 Open the box very briefly every two days to water the seedlings and observe them.

7 After about 1 week to 10 days make drawings of your seedlings in the shoebox. What do you notice about the way they are growing? What colour are their leaves and stems?

8 After 10 days one of the seedlings should begin to grow through the hole. If this does not happen, guide one seedling so that it comes through the hole.

9 After two days observe the seedling that came through the hole and draw it.

10 Compare the seedling that came through the hole and those that did not. Answer these questions with complete sentences:

a) What is the colour of the stems and leaves of the seedling that came through the hole? What is the colour of those in the box?

b) Why do you think the seedling that came through the hole became that colour?

c) Do you think the part of the seedling that came through the hole looked healthy? Compare it to the seedlings in the box.

11 Discuss with your group the effect of light on plants. When you agree, write your group's opinion in answer to **a)** to **c)**. Write complete sentences.

a) How do plants grow when they get light from one direction only?

b) How will plants look when they get no light at all? (Chapter 3 in Book 4 will help you to answer this question.)

c) What causes plants to turn green?

Project

Write three things that would happen on earth if the sun were destroyed.

Activity 2 Water and seeds

Your group will need:
- 60 red bean seeds
- a metric ruler
- a balance
- a plastic container with water
- 2 paper napkins
- a hand lens

Share materials

Look at the safety note on page 55.

1 Draw one seed from the front and the side. Label your drawing.

2 Discuss with your group what you think the white part is for.

3 Find the mass of 50 seeds. Note it down. Calculate the mass of 1 seed.

4 Place the 50 seeds in a plastic container three-quarters full with water. Leave until the next day.

5 Next day, dry the seeds gently (do not squeeze them). Find the mass of the 50 soaked seeds.

6 Make a table like Table 1 in your notebooks.

Table 1 *Mass of seeds*

No. of seeds	Mass when dry	Mass when soaked	Gain in mass
50			
1			

7 Discuss **a)** to **e)** with your group. When you all agree, write the answers in your book. Write complete sentences.

   a) Did the seeds change size when you soaked them?
   b) How much mass did the 50 seeds gain?
   c) How much mass did 1 seed gain?
   d) What caused the seeds to gain mass?
   e) How do you think the water got into the seeds?

8 Examine a soaked seed, squeeze it. While you squeeze the seed, listen to it and look at it with the hand lens. Discuss what you observe with your group.

9 Do you want to change or add to your answer for **e)** above?

10 Peel off the red seed covering with your finger nails.

11 Open the seed.
Draw and label it.
The diagram will help you.

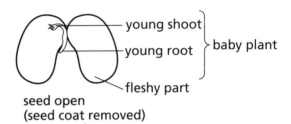

seed open
(seed coat removed)

There is a baby plant in the seed.
It needs food to germinate
(start growing).
The seed stores solid food in the
fleshy part.
Water helps to change the stored food
into a form that the baby plant can use.

Did you know?
- Scientists have found seeds over 10,000 years old. These seeds can still germinate.

Activity 3 Watering plants

Your group will need:
- **20 black-eye pea seedlings in a butter bowl**
- **2 styrofoam cups**
- **a teaspoon**
- **cotton wool or toilet paper**

Look at the safety note on page 55.

1 Your teacher will give you 20 black-eye pea seedlings in a butter bowl.

2 Label the styrofoam cups A and B. Fill each with loosely packed toilet paper or cotton wool.

3 Three days after the root grows out of the seed, carefully remove 10 seedlings (of about the same size) from the butter bowl. Be very careful not to damage the roots. Put 5 seedlings into cup A and 5 seedlings into cup B.

4 Measure out and pour 1 teaspoon (5 ml) of water into cup A. Do the same for cup B.

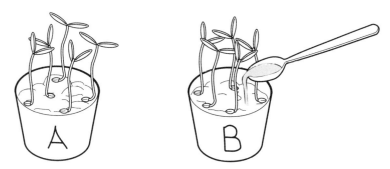

5 Every day for the next three weeks, water the seedlings in A with 1 teaspoon of water. Do your watering at the same time each day.

6 Water the seedlings in cup B with 1 teaspoon of water twice a week for the next three weeks.

7 Examine the seedlings in A and B at the end of each week.

8 Make a drawing of the seedlings at the end of the third week.

9 Discuss with your group what differences you observe between the seedlings in A and B. When you all agree, copy and complete the table below.

Table 2   How seedlings in cup A and cup B are alike and different

	Seedlings in A	Seedlings in B
Alike		
Different		

Plants need water. Plants are able to make their food by using water, carbon dioxide from the air, and light energy from the sun.

Many years ago scientists thought that plants got their food from the soil. They believed that plants did not have to make their food. Just over 300 years ago a Belgian medical doctor, Van Helmont, showed that plants use water to form their food. Plants therefore need water.

Plants also need water to keep their stems upright and their leaves open to catch the sunlight. Water makes stems and leaves stiff. Without water plants wilt and will eventually die.

Communicating

Summary

- If you grow plants in a dark area with light coming from one direction only, their stems will bend and grow toward the light source.
- Plants become green when you expose them to light. Plants must be green in order to make their food. Because they can make their own food, green plants are at the beginning of every food chain.
- Seeds will not germinate until they get enough water to change stored food into a soluble form that the embryo can use to grow and develop.
- When a seed takes in water, it becomes larger and its mass increases. The seed coat softens and the root and shoot grow out.
- When the fleshy parts of a seedling no longer have food stored they wither. The green leaves of the seedling take over making food for the young plant.
- Water in the stems and leaves of plants keeps the plant body and leaves stiff. Without water the plant wilts and eventually dies.

Test yourself ✏

For each task write down **A**, **B**, **C** or **D** and give a reason for your answer.

Use the diagram below for tasks 1 and 2.

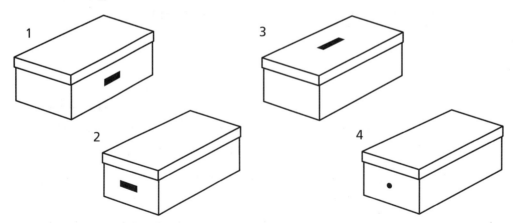

1 The dark area of each box represents a hole cut out. The boxes are black inside. A three-day-old lentil seedling was placed in the middle of each box. The seedling that grew without bending was in box

   A 1   **B** 2   **C** 3   **D** 4

(Objective 1)

2 The seedlings in boxes 1, 2, 3 and 4 above all grew toward

  A water

  B earth

  C a warm area

  D light

(Objective 1)

3 Seeds kept in an area without water will

  A die

  B not germinate

  C crack up

  D germinate

(Objective 2)

4 Isabel put 25 seeds in a glass of water and left them overnight. The next day she found that the seeds

  A drowned

  B got larger

  C became green

  D sent out leaves

(Objective 2)

5 The seed coat in each of Isabel's seeds got

  A soft

  B lighter in colour

  C green

  D hard

(Objective 2)

6 Harry grew some seedlings in a butter bowl on cotton wool. He kept the butter bowl near to a pond with water. He did not water the seedlings for 5 days. The stems of the seedlings

  A grew toward the pond with water

  B became yellow

  C wilted

  D cracked up

(Objective 3)

Communicating

7 Seedlings need water
   A for making food
   B for the animals that eat them to get water
   C for the water cycle
   D to keep them cool

(Objective 3)

Help each
other

Re-using

Objectives

At the end of the chapter pupils should be able to

1 design and construct useful items from discarded objects (pages 64–65)

2 describe the construction details of the useful items (page 64)

3 describe and demonstrate how the items may be made (pages 64–65).

In these activities we are going to make new and useful things from old items that people usually throw away. By re-using items we save our parents' money. We can save our government money too. If we re-use things we throw less away. This means the garbage collections will have fewer pick-ups and use less gas. The land-fills will take longer to fill up.

Imagine you are going to make something useful to sell at a school bazaar. The following activity will help you to plan, design and make something new from something old. You can use this knowledge to make other items.

Problems should be solved by the group

Communicating

Activity 1 Making a paper bag

Your group will need:
- various types of scrap paper (e.g. newspaper, used computer paper, old notebooks, etc.)
- old paper bags (store bags, grocery bags, etc.)
- glue
- scissors
- cardboard from a shoebox
- string
- water colour paints
- paint brushes
- a ruler

Your task is to make a paper bag from re-usable paper. The bag must be large enough and strong enough to hold things.

1 Look at as many paper bags as you can. Take them apart and discuss with your group how they are made. This is your research.

2 When your group has decided on a design for your bag, make drawings to help you make it. It may be a combination of different bag designs.

3 Discuss the steps of the simple design opposite. It will help you to improve the drawings of your own design.

4 Make the bag according to your group's plan.

5 Discuss what you will write on your bag and how you will decorate it.

6 Decide what your bag will be used for. Test its strength and size.

7 If your bag is not strong enough or large enough then you must look at your design again and see if you can improve it.

8 Prepare a report to read to the rest of the class. You should explain your design, how the bag may be used, how strong it is, how pretty it is and why people should want to buy it at the bazaar.

1 Your paper should look like this but longer.

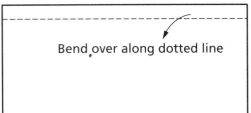

Bend over along dotted line

2 Bend along (a) and along (b). Put glue at the back of (c).

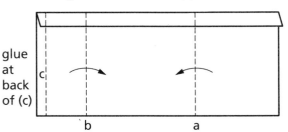

glue at back of (c)

c

b   a

3

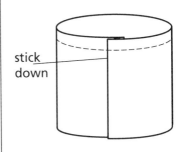

stick down

4 Flatten 3. Cut out (d) and (e).

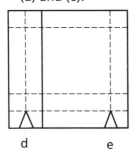

d   e

5 Bend forward and backward along (f) and (g) and crease each time.

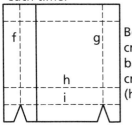

f   g

h
i

Bend up and crease. Bend back and crease along (h) and (i).

6 Push in sides.

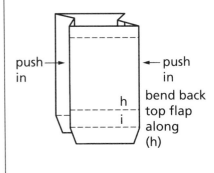

push in   push in

bend back top flap along (h)

h
i

7 Top flap bent back along (h).

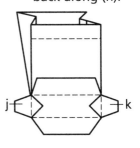

j   k

8 Bend in (j) and (k).

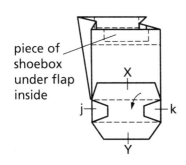

piece of shoebox under flap inside

X

j   k

Y

9 Bend over (X). Mark areas on (j) and (k) to apply glue. Bend up (Y) along (i). Mark area for gluing on (X).

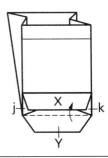

j   X   k

Y

10 Glue (X) on (j) and (k). Glue (Y) on (j) and (k) and on lower part of (X).

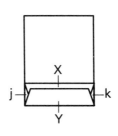

X

j   k

Y

11 Bore holes and insert strings.

Stick piece of shoebox at base of bag

Communicating

Summary

- When we re-use an item, we extend its life. To do this we may repair it, modify it or create new uses for it.
- In this chapter we found new uses for paper which people throw away. In order to do this we researched, planned, made, and tested our design. Use these processes when you decide to make something.

Test yourself performance assessment

Each group can select another item to make for the school bazaar. Use the processes used when you made your paper bag.

1 'A desk tidy' for holding pens, pencils, paperclips, etc. Collect toilet rolls, old Christmas gift paper, glue, a shoebox and anything else your group may need.

2 'Attractive writing paper'. Collect notebook pages, water colour paints, brush or straw, perfume and anything else your group may need.

3 'Labels for preserved fruit'. Collect paper scraps from a commercial printers, coloured markers, etc.

4 'Gift wrapping paper'. Collect scraps of paper, crayons, leaves, flowers, paint, etc.

Mystery Boxes

Objectives

At the end of the chapter pupils should be able to

1   make inferences about mystery boxes by shaking them, feeling them, listening to objects moving in them or by using a magnet (pages 67–69).

In this chapter you will make observations about objects you cannot see. You will then use these observations to say what you think the unseen objects are. When you do this you are making an **inference**. An inference is not just a guess, you need to produce observations to support your inference.

A doctor listens to a patient's heart beat with a stethoscope and may infer that the patient has an enlarged heart. He/she may listen to the patient's breathing and infer that the air tubes in the lungs are slightly clogged. The doctor has made inferences from his/her observations.

Activity 1 Getting to know the objects

Your group will need:

- a magnet
- 6 objects for the mystery box:
  a ping-pong ball
  a ball from a roll-on deodorant
  wooden block or plastic block
  metal jar lid
  scented soap (toilet soap)
  plastic jar lid

> Bring materials to class when asked

1   Pass each object listed above around the class. Discuss with your group how the objects are alike and how they are different.

2   How could you know one from the other if each object was in a separate closed box? Answer these questions to help you.

   a) What do balls do?
   b) How could you tell the difference between the ping-pong ball and the deodorant ball?

c) How could you identify the soap in a box?

d) How could you use the magnet to identify any of the objects?

e) How could you tell the difference between the plastic lid and the metal lid, the plastic block and the wooden block?

3 Write down your observations in your notebooks.

Activity 2 Mystery boxes

Your group will need:

• a magnet
• objects listed in Activity 1
• 6 shoeboxes

1 Your teacher will place six closed shoeboxes with an object in each on some desks. The boxes are marked 1 to 6.

2 Go to each box in turn. Each member of the group will tilt the box, shake the box, smell the box, listen for sounds, lift the box.

3 Write down your observations in a table like Table 1 below. Discuss with your group what inference you can make from these observations. When you all agree, write down your inference in your table.

4 Move to the next box when your teacher taps the desk after about 3 or 4 minutes. Write down your observations and inferences for every mystery box in your table.

Table 1

Box no.	Inference	Observations that support our inferences
1		
2		
3		

5 Remember that your inference is only good if your observations support your inference. Sign your work and show your teacher.

Summary

- When we infer we try to explain or give reasons for observations we make about objects or events which we cannot actually see.
- When you make an inference it is important that you state the observations you made with your senses to support your inference.
- Inferences are not facts, they may change as a result of new evidence or further observations.
- A good inference is one which is well supported by your observations.

Test Yourself

For each task write down **A**, **B**, **C** or **D**.

1 Miss Seeta gave Carissa and Yusuff two closed boxes. She told them there was a steel cover in one and a plastic cover in the other. They lifted the boxes, they shook them and listened to the contents rolling. They could not say which was which. The children should

   A shake them again   **B** use a magnet

   C open the box   **D** guess

                                           (Objective 1)

2 Miss Seeta gave Ryan and Kerenzia two sealed boxes. She told them one had a toilet soap, the other had a block of wood. In order to make a reasonable inference about which is which they should

   A guess   **B** ask someone

   C open the boxes   **D** smell the boxes

                                             (Objective 1)

3 Mr James gave two pupils two boxes. He told them one had a tennis ball and the other a ping-pong ball. In order to make a reasonable inference about which is which they should

   A bounce the boxes   **B** smell the boxes

   C lift the boxes   **D** squeeze the boxes

                                             (Objective 1)

Chapter 12

Effect of Temperature on Dissolving Time

Objectives

At the end of the chapter pupils should be able to

1 predict whether a solid will dissolve faster as the temperature increases (pages 70–72)

2 identify the sequence on a graph that predicts the dissolving time of a solid as temperature is increased (page 72).

In this chapter a teaspoon of sugar means a teaspoon with a level sugar surface. To dissolve the sugar (solute) you must stir the water until you can no longer see the sugar and it does not settle out.

You will collect data and plot the data on a graph. You will observe the pattern the graph makes and use it to make predictions about the time it takes to dissolve sugar at different temperatures.

Activity 1 Dissolving time

Your group will need:
- a thermometer
- a bowl of brown sugar
- ice
- hot water (supplied by your teacher in a thermos flask)
- watch with a second hand
- 2 styrofoam cups: A (9 cm tall) and B (13 cm tall)
- a teaspoon
- a straw
- graph paper
- a ruler
- a sheet of old newspaper to spread on your desk

Safety!
- Do not eat the sugar or the ice.

1 Draw a line with a pencil on the inside of cup A, 4 cm up from the bottom. Draw a line 10 cm from the bottom of cup B.

2 Put tap water up to the 10 cm mark in cup B. Add ice and stir with the straw. Keep checking the temperature with your thermometer until it reaches 10°C.

3 Pour water at 10°C into cup A until it reaches the 4 cm mark.

4 Quickly put a teaspoon of sugar into cup A. Note the time. Stir the water until the sugar dissolves. Note the time when it has completely dissolved.

5 Throw out the solution from cup A. Rinse the cup.

Take turns answering questions

6 Record your data in a table like Table 1.

Table 1

Temperature of water (in °C)	Time to dissolve 1 teaspoon of sugar (seconds)			
	Trial 1	Trial 2	Trial 3	Average (or mean)
10				
20				
40				
50				

7 Repeat steps 2 to 6 two more times. Find the *average* time taken to dissolve the sugar in water at 10°C. Enter your average in column 5.

8 Remove or add ice to cup B and add water up to the 10 cm mark. Use your thermometer to observe when the temperature reaches 20°C.

9 Pour water at 20°C into cup A until it reaches the 4 cm mark.

10 Repeat steps 4 to 6 three times using water at 20°C.

11 Find the average dissolving time of the sugar at 20°C and enter the average in your table.

12 Prepare water at 40°C and 50°C by adding some warm water to cup B. Find the dissolving time of sugar at that temperature. Do this three times so that you can find an average time and enter this in your table.

13 Discuss Table 1 with your group. Discuss why you needed to find an average time for sugar dissolving at each temperature.

14 Plot the data in Table 1 on a graph like the one below.

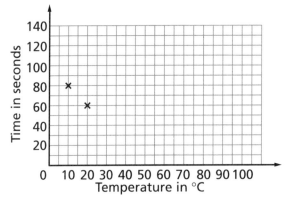

15 Discuss with your group how you can use your graph to predict how long it will take to dissolve a teaspoon of sugar
   a) at room temperature, b) at 60°C and c) at 15°C.
   Write down your predictions in your notebook.

16 Predict at what temperature a teaspoon of sugar will dissolve in 90 minutes.

17 Dissolve a teaspoon of sugar at room temperature. Time how long it takes for the sugar to dissolve. Is it close to what you predicted?

Summary

- Some solids dissolve in water. The solid is the solute and the water is the solvent.
- When sugar dissolves in water we can no longer see the sugar, and the sugar will not settle out.
- Most solids dissolve faster as we increase the temperature of the solvent. That is, the dissolving time decreases as temperature increases.
- We can measure the dissolving time of a certain amount of a solid and use the data to draw a graph.
- We can use the pattern formed by the graph to predict the dissolving time of a given amount of a solid.

Test yourself ✎

For each task write down **A**, **B**, **C** or **D** and give a reason for your answer.

1 Some pupils plotted this graph when they dissolved 45 ml of salt in water at different temperatures.

The graph shows that

   A salt dissolves faster than sugar

   B the dissolving time for salt increases

   C when the temperature increases the salt dissolves faster

   D the dissolving time decreases as the temperature decreases

(Objectives 1 and 2)

2 Which graph shows that the dissolving time of a solute decreases with an increase in temperature of the solvent?

A

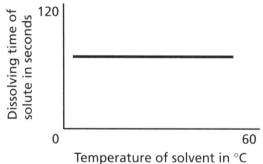

B

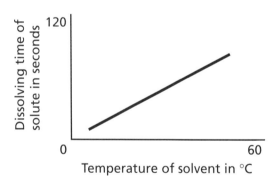

C

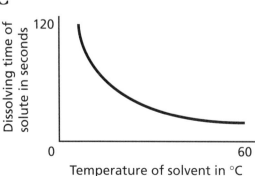

D

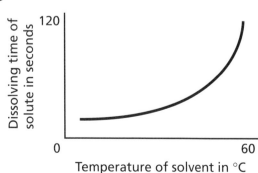

(Objective 2)

3

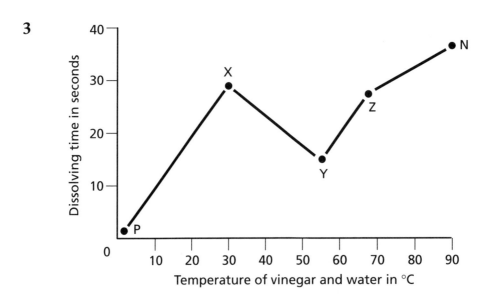

Some of the points on this graph have been plotted wrongly.
The part of the line in the graph which correctly shows that baking
soda in water and vinegar dissolves faster as the temperature
increases is

A XY **B** YZ **C** ZN **D** PX

(Objective 2)

4 A certain amount of a solute will dissolve in 50 ml of a solvent at
20°C in 72 seconds. At 80°C it takes 14 seconds to dissolve. At 60°C
the same solute will dissolve in the same solvent in

A 2 seconds **B** 12 seconds **C** 25 seconds **D** 80 seconds

(Objective 1)

5 Sitara and Hatim drink Ovaltine at breakfast. Hatim likes his
Ovaltine cold. Sitara likes hers hot. Sitara says her Ovaltine will
dissolve faster in hot water. Hatim says it will dissolve faster in cold
water. After they mixed their Ovaltine they were able to conclude that

A Sitara was right

B Hatim was right

C neither was right

D the statements cannot be tested

(Objective 1)

Temperature Change

> ## Objectives
>
> At the end of the chapter pupils should be able to
>
> 1 predict the temperature of a mixture of equal volumes of hot and cold water of known temperature (pages 75–77)
>
> 2 predict the temperature of a mixture of unequal volumes of hot and cold water (pages 77–78).

Jack mixed his tea and took a sip. Splatt! Out of his mouth it came. It was too hot. Jill told him to add some cold water. Jack did. Did the tea become cooler? How much cooler? Let's find out.

Activity 1 Oh! My tea is too hot

Your group will need:
- 3 styrofoam cups (one must be larger than the other two)
- pencil
- ruler
- ice (provided by the teacher in a thermos flask)
- warm water (in a thermos flask)
- thermometer
- 100 ml measuring cylinder

Safety!
- Be careful with the warm water.

1 Label the two small cups A and B. Label the large cup C.

2 Pour water into the measuring cylinder until it reaches the 50 ml mark.

3 Pour the water into cup A. Draw a mark on the cup to show where the water level is. Do the same with cup B.

4 Pour warm water into cups A and B up to the 50 ml line.

5 Measure the temperature of the water in cups A and B. Record the data in a table like Table 1.

6 Quickly pour the water from cups A and B into cup C. Measure the temperature in cup C right away. Record it in your table.

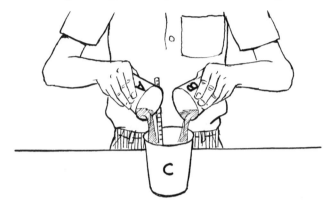

Table 1

	Temperature in °C		
	Cup A 50 ml water	Cup B 50 ml water	Cup C 100 ml water
Trial 1 (warm + warm water)			
Trial 2 (cold + cold water)			
Trial 3 (warm + cold water)			

7 Throw away the water.

8 Repeat steps 4 to 7 using cold water in cups A and B.

9 Pour warm water into cup A and cold water into cup B up to the 50 ml line in each cup.

10 Measure the temperature of the water in cups A and B and record the data on your table. While some of the group are doing this, let the others answer the question in step 11.

11 If you mix all the water in cup A with the water in cup B, what temperature do you think the mixture will be? Write your prediction in your notebook.

12 Quickly pour the water from cups A and B into cup C. Measure the temperature of the water in cup C. Record the data in Table 1.

13 Was your prediction very good, good, not so good?

14 Compare the temperatures of the water in cups A and B with the mixture of the waters in cup C.

15 Try out some more tests with 50 ml of water at different temperatures and then copy and complete the following sentence.

> When I mix equal amounts of hot and cold water, the temperature of the mixed water is _____ of the two temperatures.

16 Was the temperature of the mixture of warm and cold water near the average of the temperature of the warm water and the temperature of the cold water in each case? Work out the averages and see.

17 Discuss with your group why the temperature of the mixture was not *exactly* equal to the average. When you all agree, write one or two sentences to explain it.

Were any of the experiments in the last activity like Jack's tea and water mixing?

Activity 2 Mixing different volumes of water at different temperatures

Your group will need:
* the same materials as Activity 1

Look at the safety note on page 75.

1 Rub out the pencil mark in cup B.

2 Pour water into the measuring cylinder up to the 75 ml mark. Now pour the water into cup B and make a mark.

3 Pour warm water into cup A up to the 50 ml line. Pour cold water into cup B up to the 75 ml line.

Predicting

Table 2

	Temperature in °C		
	Cup A 50 ml water	Cup B 75 ml water	Cup C 125 ml water
Trial 1 (warm + cold water)			

4 Measure the temperature of the water in cups A and B. Record the data in a table like Table 2.

5 If you mix all the water from cup A with all the water from cup B, what temperature do you think the mixture will be? Write your prediction in your notebook.

6 Quickly pour the water from cups A and B into cup C. Measure the temperature in cup C. Record the data in your table. Was your prediction good, very good or not so good?

7 Discuss with your group how the temperature of the water in cup C compares with the temperature of the water in cups A and B.

8 Copy and complete the sentence below.

> When we mix two unequal volumes of water at different temperatures, the temperature of the mixture is nearer to the one with the _____ volume.

Summary

- When we mix two equal volumes of water of different temperatures, we can predict that the temperature of the resulting mixture will be the average of the two temperatures.
- If we mix two unequal volumes of water of different temperatures, we can predict that the temperature of the resulting mixture will be nearer to the temperature of the greater volume of water.

Test yourself

For each task write down **A**, **B**, **C** or **D** and give a reason for your answer.

1 A cup with 50 ml of water at 60°C was mixed with 50 ml of water at 20°C. The resulting temperature of the mixture was

   A 20°C   **B** 40°C   **C** 60°C   **D** 80°C

(Objective 1)

2 A boy mixed 50 ml of water at 60°C with 50 ml of water at 40°C. He should predict the resulting mixture of the water to be at

   A 40°C   **B** 50°C   **C** 60°C   **D** 100°C

(Objective 1)

3 Mary mixed 40 ml of water at 10°C with 200 ml of tea at 94°C. The resulting temperature was

   A 10°C   **B** 52°C   **C** 80°C   **D** 94°C

Give a reason for your choice.

(Objective 2)

4 Your teacher mixed 2000 ml of water at 4°C with 25 ml of water at 100°C. You predict the resulting mixture of the water to be at

   A 5°C   **B** 52°C   **C** 84°C   **D** 104°C

Give a reason for your choice.

5 Two students mixed 80 ml of water at 30°C with 20 ml of water at 60°C. Mary predicted that the temperature of the mixture would be the average of 30°C and 60°C. Harry predicted that the temperature of the mixture would be nearer 60°C than 30°C.

   A Mary's prediction is correct

   B Harry's prediction is correct

   C Both Mary's and Harry's predictions are correct

   D Neither Mary's nor Harry's prediction is correct

Give a reason for your choice.

(Objective 2)

Observing

6 (Group work)

Trial	Temperature in °C		
	Cup A 60 ml water	Cup B 40 ml water	Cup C (mixture) 100 ml water
1	70	70	
2	50	50	
3	40	40	
4	20	76	

a) Each member of your group must perform one of the trials in the table above.

b) Pool your group's results. Copy and complete the table.

c) Discuss the table with your group. Make a general statement about mixing unequal volumes of water (e.g. 60 ml and 40 ml) at the same temperature. When you all agree, copy and complete this statement:

When unequal volumes of water at the same temperature are mixed, the temperature of the mixture _____.

(Performance assessment)

Living Things

> ## Objectives
>
> At the end of the chapter pupils should be able to
>
> 1 use a given operational definition to identify plants and animals as living (pages 81–85)
>
> 2 use an operational definition to distinguish between living things and non-living things (page 86).

An **operational definition** of plants and animals as living things must tell us what living plants and animals do and what we observe about them.

What grows?

Here is an operational definition of a living thing:

• When living things are placed in a suitable environment they **grow**.

Try the following activity to see whether seeds and stones are living or non-living things.

Activity 1　Do seeds and stones grow?

Your group will need:
• black-eye peas
• stones
• soil
• 2 styrofoam cups

1 Label the cups A and B and fill them three-quarters full with soil.

2 Place the seeds on top of the soil in cup A and then cover them with more soil.

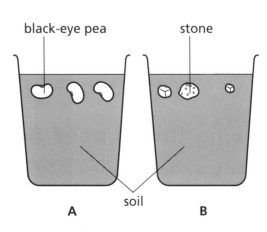

3 Repeat step 2 with cup B, using some stones instead of seeds.

4 Water each cup every day and leave them in a sunny place.

5 Predict what you think will happen to the seeds and stones in a few days' time.

6 Observe what happens to the stones and seeds.

7 Did the seeds grow? Why? Did the stones grow? Why?

Activity 2   Do animals grow?

1 Look at the pictures.

2 Do the kitten, baby and toy doll grow?

3 Draw what the kitten, baby and doll will look like in 5 years' time.

4 Discuss with your group whether the baby, kitten and doll are living.

5 Are the baby and kitten animals or plants?

People do not always think of themselves as animals but in science we define humans as animals.

Plants and animals grow. They are living things.

Living things need air

Here is another operational definition:
• Living things **take in air**. Without air living things die.

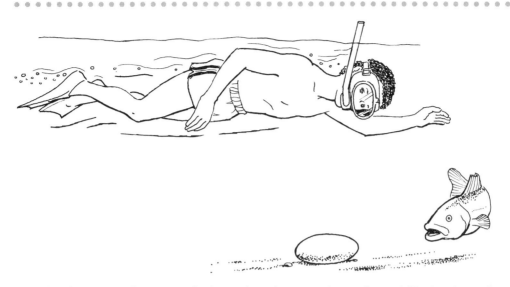

1 The boy needs a snorkel so that he can breathe while he is swimming underwater. He could not survive without air.

2 Does the fish need air? The fish can breathe underwater because it takes in air from the water through its gills. The air is dissolved in the water.

3 Does the stone need air?

In Chapter 3 of Book 4 you learned that plants need air. You may have done an activity that showed that seeds will not germinate if they have no air.

Plants use air to help make their food. Plants cannot grow on the moon. There is no air and no water on the moon.

Living things need food

Here is another operational definition:
• Living things **need food** to stay alive and to grow and develop.

Activity 3 Whose food?

1 Your teacher will give you some red bean seeds which were soaked in water overnight.
2 Remove the seed coat. Look for the baby plant.
3 Draw the baby plant in your notebook.
4 Draw the two fleshy parts in your book.
5 Discuss with your group which part of the bean is food for the baby plant. Which part of the bean is food for the children? When you all agree, write the answers in your book.
6 Do plants and animals need food?

Living things can move

Here is another operational definition:
• Living things can **move** by themselves, while non-living things cannot.
Look at the pictures.

Is the lion moving? Is the person moving?
Does the plant move? Does the stone move?

Animals move from place to place in search of food. The lion hunts the deer. People go to the shops for food. Plants move very little because they can make their own food. But they need light and water to make food so their stems and their leaves bend towards light. Their roots bend towards water and towards the earth.

Living things get rid of waste

Here is another operational definition:
• Living things **get rid of waste** while non-living things do not.

Living plants get rid of waste. They drop their yellow leaves.
Animals too get rid of waste.

Living things reproduce

Here is another operational definition:
* Living things **reproduce** (produce young ones). The young ones
  usually look like their parents.

1 Where does the puppy come from?

2 Where does the baby come from?

3 Does the little rock come out of the big rock?

Which of these things are living things?

Defining operationally

Living or non-living

Discuss the list of things below with your group. Copy and complete the table by placing a ✔ for **yes** and a ✗ for **no** under each column. Decide which are living and which are non-living. The first one has been done for you.

Table 1

Organism	Grows	Moves	Reproduces	Needs air	Needs food	Gets rid of waste	Living	Animal	Plant
Spider	✔	✔	✔	✔	✔	✔	✔	✔	
Worm									
Grass									
Boy									
Snail									
Fire									
Whale									
Car									
Carrot									
Cloud									

Summary
- An operational definition tells us what is done and what we observe.
- We can identify living things by the following characteristics or traits. Living things grow, reproduce, move, need food, need air and get rid of waste.
- Plants and animals are living things because they grow, reproduce, move, need food, need air and get rid of waste. Non-living things cannot do these things.

Test yourself

For each task write down **A**, **B**, **C** or **D** and give a reason for your answer.

Use the information given by this definition and the list of organisms for tasks 1, 2 and 3.

Plants and animals are living things. They grow, reproduce, move, need food and air and get rid of waste.

grass   carrot   worm   man   caterpillar

1 The organisms in the list above that are living things are

    A man and worm only

    B man and caterpillar only

    C worm, man and caterpillar only

    D all of them

(Objectives 1 and 2)

2 The organisms in the list above that are animals are

    A worm and caterpillar only

    B worm, man and caterpillar only

    C grass, carrot and worm only

    D carrot, worm and man only

(Objective 2)

3 The organisms in the list above that are plants are

    A grass, carrot and worm only

    B carrot and worm only

    C grass and carrot only

    D man and caterpillar only

(Objective 1)

Use this list to answer question 4

cloud   boy   moving car   fire   seed   carrot

4 The living things in the list are

    A cloud, boy and moving car   **B** boy, moving car and fire

    C boy, moving car and seed   **D** boy, seed and carrot

(Objectives 1 and 2)

Floating and Sinking

Objectives

At the end of the chapter pupils should be able to

1 observe that some objects float and some sink in water (pages 88–89)

2 construct an operational definition for floating and sinking (page 89).

Activity 1 Which objects float?

Your group will need:
- pencil
- small blown-up round balloon
- styrofoam tray
- styrofoam block
- stone
- a straw
- wooden block
- piece of candle
- marble
- ping-pong ball or deodorant ball
- nail
- pail with water
- lump of plasticine
- ruler

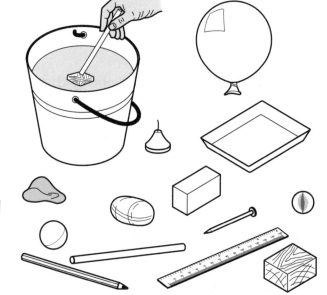

1 Discuss with your group which objects will sink and which will float. When you all agree, prepare a table like Table 1 below and fill in columns 1 and 2.

Table 1

Object	We think the object will float (yes/no)	The object floated (yes/no)	Force of water pushing up (strong/weak)
Pencil			
Balloon			

2 Put each object in turn in the water. Complete column 3 of Table 1.

3 Use the straw to push each object that floats down into the water. Then release it. Did you feel the water pushing the object up?

4 Discuss with your group which items the water pushed up with a strong force. When you all agree, complete your column 4.

5 Discuss with your group what you observed about the water force on the items that float. When you all agree copy and complete the operational definition below.

---

a) When we push down an object in water and the water _____ with a great force, the object will float.

b) When we push down an object in water and the water does not _____ the object will _____.

c) When we push down an object in water and it does not _____ it is a sinker

d) When we push down an object in water and _____ it is a floater.

Activity 2

Your group will need:
- a small inflated round balloon
- a metal lid from an Ovaltine tin
- a stone
- a candle
- a pail with water

1 Put the tin cover gently on the surface of the water. Does it float? Is it a floater or a sinker?

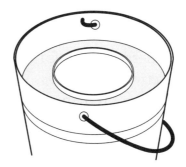

2 Push down the tin cover in the water to the bottom of the container. Release it.

Defining operationally

3 Discuss 5 **c)** and **d)** of Activity 1 with your group. When you all agree, write in your books whether you think the tin cover is a sinker or a floater. Give a reason for your group's decision.

4 Repeat steps 1 and 3 with the other objects.

5 Hold the balloon by the neck. Pull it down completely under the water surface. Write a sentence about pulling the balloon under the water.

6 Marine engineers use large balloons to bring up parts of sunken boats from under the sea. Discuss this with your group. Write a short paragraph about how you think this is done and why it is possible.

Activity 3   Salt water/fresh water floating?

Your group will need:
- about 100 ml of tap water in a plastic container
- 2 Cheers plastic cylinders labelled A and B
- lead pencil about 15 cm long with eraser
- about 2 teaspoons of table salt
- measuring cylinder (optional)
- ruler
- an egg

1 Pour water from the plastic container into cylinder A up to 11 cm deep (30 ml).

2 Add one teaspoon of salt to the water left in the container. Stir until all the salt dissolves.

3 Pour salt water into cylinder B up to 11 cm.

4 Place the pencil into cylinder A. Measure the distance from the water line to the top of the pencil. Take a note of it.

5 Repeat 4 using cylinder B with the salt water.

6 Read your operational definition at 5 **a)** and **b)** in Activity 1. Discuss what took place in 4 and 5 in this Activity with your group. When you all agree write a sentence about the pushing-up force of the water in A and B.

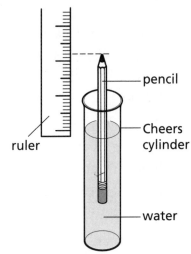

ruler

pencil

Cheers cylinder

water

7 Discuss with your group what you think will happen if you place an egg in a glass of tap water, and then in a glass of salt water. When you all agree, write what you predict and give a reason.

8 Perform the task. Was your prediction very good, good, not so good?

Summary

- Some things float in water. Some things sink in water.
- When you push an object down in water, the water pushes up on the object. If the push-up force of the water is great the object floats. If the push-up force of the water is small, the object sinks.
- If you push an object to the bottom of a container of water and it stays there the object is a sinker. If the object comes back up it is a floater.
- Salt water has a greater push-up force on objects placed in it than tap water has. Some objects that sink in tap water may float in salt water.

Test yourself

For each task write down **A**, **B**, **C** or **D** and give a reason for your answer.

Use the diagram to answer tasks 1 and 2.

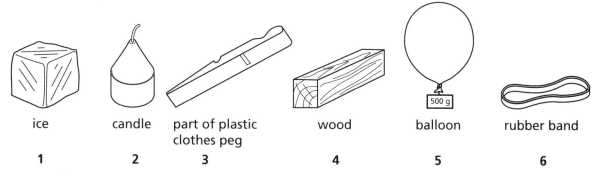

ice	candle	part of plastic clothes peg	wood	balloon	rubber band
1	2	3	4	5	6

1 The items that will float in the diagram above are

    A 1, 2 and 3   **C** 1, 2, 3, 4 and 5

    B 1, 2, 3 and 4   **D** 1,2, 3, 4, 5 and 6

                                                     (Objective 1)

2 The item/s that will sink in the diagram above is/are

    A 1, 2 and 3   **C** 4 and 5

    B 2, 3 and 4·   **D** 6 only

                                                     (Objective 1)

3 Below are two operational definitions made by Indra and Kirk.

Indra: 'If you push an object to the bottom of a tank of water, and it comes back to the top and stays when you release it, it is a floater.'

Kirk: 'If you push an object to the bottom of a tank of water, and it stays at the bottom when you release it, it is a sinker.'

An operational definition was made by

A Indra only   **C** both Indra and Kirk

B Kirk only   **D** Neither Kirk nor Indra

(Objective 2)

4 Get a piece of candle about 11 cm long and 2 cm diameter, and a piece of plasticine about the same size. Find the weight of each in air and in water in force units. Prepare a table like the one below. If your spring balance is graduated in grams, ignore grams and write force units (weight is a force and is not measured in grams).

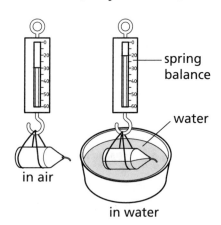

spring balance

water

in air

in water

Table 2

Item	Sink or float	Weight in air in force units (X)	Weight in water in force units (Y)	Push-up force of water in force units (X–Y)
Candle				
Plasticine				

Which item did the water push up with a greater force? Write an operational definition of sinking and floating. Make use of the push-up force of water. Remember an operational definition says what you do and what you observe.

(Performance assessment)

Revision Test

For each question, write down **A, B, C** or **D**.

1 Having too many grazing animals on the land can cause erosion of the soil because the animals

   A splash water on the soil   **B** kick up and loosen the soil
      when bathing
   C eat the cover crops   **D** trample the soil

2 You can make a soil absorb more water, and thus reduce the amount of erosion, by adding to the soil

   A clay   **B** sand   **C** humus   **D** white lime

3 Energy from the sun turns into heat energy when it strikes material that absorbs it. The colour of the material that absorbs the energy best is

   A red   **B** black   **C** yellow   **D** blue

4 A balloon is fitted into each of two bottles as shown in the diagram. There is a hole at the bottom of bottle B. When two pupils blow air into bottles A and B, the result is that

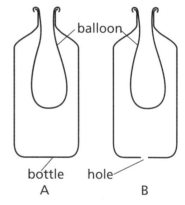

   A both balloons fill with air
   B neither balloon fills with air
   C only the balloon in A fills with air
   D only the balloon in B fills with air
Give a reason for your choice.

5 Carissa spent the weekend at the beach and brought some sea water to school. What could she do to make it pure water?

   A Boil the water   **B** Evaporate and collect the water
   C Filter the water   **D** Decant the water

6 The input gear of the egg beater in the diagram is at

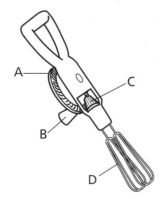

   A
   B
   C
   D

7 A student put 28 drops of tap water on a 25¢ coin. The water bulged over the sides and rose high up over the coin. Another student used water with some liquid soap in it. The water remained flat on the coin and ran off after 12 drops were added. This happened because

A the soap broke the surface tension links
B the soap made the coin slippery
C silver coins repel soapy water
D the second student put larger drops on

8 A housewife who washes her clothes in rainwater spends less money buying soap than one who uses tap water because

A rainwater is soft water and softens clothes
B tap water is hard water and does not soften clothes
C rainwater washes whiter than tap water
D rainwater is soft water and lathers easily

9 Which of the following is re-using?

A scrap iron from old cans melted down and used to make new cans
B old tyres tied to the side of a jetty as a cushion for boats
C dead plants put back into the soil to decay
D scrap lead melted down and used to make batteries

Give a reason for your answer.

10 Pablo grew two well-watered lentil seedlings in similar dark boxes, X and Y. Box X had a hole in the side of it. After three days Pablo opened both boxes and saw the seedlings as in the diagram.

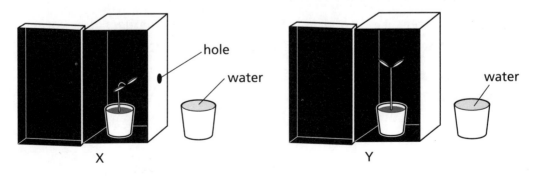

Pablo should conclude that

A plants bend easily when young   **B** plants do not grow in the dark
C plants grow towards water   **D** plants grow towards light

11 All the water from the two measuring cylinders was poured into the beaker. The temperature was taken immediately and found to be

A 10 °C   **B** 26 °C   **C** 50 °C   **D** 90 °C

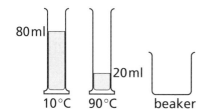

12 Carissa dissolved two tablets in each of the cylinders in the diagram.

She noted the time they took to dissolve completely. She drew this graph:

The graph shows that

A the increase in temperature does not affect dissolving time

B as temperature increases dissolving time decreases

C as temperature increases dissolving time increases

D as temperature decreases dissolving time decreases

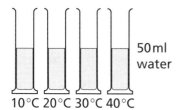

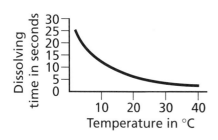

13 Michael says that a cloud is a living thing because it moves.

Anielle says that a fire is a living thing because it grows bigger and bigger.

A Only Anielle is wrong

B Only Michael is wrong

C Neither Michael nor Anielle is wrong

D Both Michael and Anielle are wrong

14 Here are two statements:

Statement 1: If you place an object in a liquid and push it down to the bottom and the object comes back up and stays on the surface of the liquid, the object is a floater.

Statement 2: If you place an object in a liquid and push it down and the liquid pushes up the object with a great force, the object will float.

From your knowledge of sinking and floating

A statement 1 is wrong

B statement 2 is wrong

C neither statement 1 nor statement 2 is wrong

D both statements are wrong

Glossary

dissolve When one component of a mixture (the solute) breaks up into particles so small that you can no longer see them in the other component (the solvent), we say that the solute has dissolved in the solvent. (page 21)

decanting If two liquids or a liquid and a solid separate into layers when they are mixed together, the top layer can be poured off. This method of separating is called decanting. (page 22)

humus Decayed dead bodies of plants and animals. It is dark in colour and found in topsoil. It is good for plant growth. It stores water well. (page 9)

insulating material Of heat – material through which heat does not pass easily. Of electricity – material through which an electric current does not pass easily. (page 17)

recycle To process manufactured materials into new forms that can be used to make new products. (page 51)

re-use To extend the life of items by repairing, modifying or finding new uses for them. (page 51)

solar energy Energy produced by the sun. (page 12)

topsoil The top part of the soil. It may be a few centimetres to more than 30 centimetres deep. It normally contains fine particles. It is usually dark in colour because it contains humus. (page 8)

transported soil Washed away soil, usually washed from higher regions to lower regions. (page 8)

solution A mixture in which no individual particles are evident. The components can be separated only by evaporation. (page 21)

suspension A mixture in which individual particles may be identified and separated by straining, filtering, decanting or by using a magnet if one of the components is magnetic. (page 22)